FACING GIANTS

Turning Opposition into Opportunity

Nick Laughter

AuthorHouse™
1663 Liberty Drive
Bloomington, IN 47403
www.authorhouse.com
Phone: 1-800-839-8640

© 2009 Nick Laughter. All rights reserved.

No part of this book may be reproduced, stored in a retrieval system, or transmitted by any means without the written permission of the author.

First published by AuthorHouse 6/02/2009

Turning Opposition into Opportunity

Nick Laughter

Scripture quotations in this book are taken from the Holman Christian Standard Bible, Copyright © 1999, 2000, 2002, 2003, 2005 by Holman Bible Publishers.

The following versions of the Bible are also used:

Verses are also taken from the New International Version®, Copyright © 1973, 1979, 1984, by the International Bible Society. Published by Zondervan Bible Publishers.

Cover design by AuthorHouse Publishing

Front cover photo from IStock Photo

ISBN: 978-1-4389-3993-3 (sc)
Printed in the United States of America
Bloomington, Indiana

This book is printed on acid-free paper.

ACKNOWLEDGMENTS

As I reflect on the completion of this project, I wish to thank the many people who have helped make my vision a reality.

Thanks first go to my parents, grandparents, and all my relatives for encouraging me to have faith and be the best I could be.

To my friends and co-workers for keeping me focused on my dreams.

To all the behind-the-scenes folk who helped me and answered my many questions-Thanks!

To all the wonderful people, great teachers, and authors who have influenced my life, belief, strategy and skill – thank you for letting me stand on your shoulders.

To everyone else who has had an impact on my life – thank you. You've helped make me who I am. I couldn't have done this without you.

Last, but definitely not least, thank you to Jesus for giving me new life, a future and a hope. May He continue to mold me into the man He planned for me to become.

Dedicated to the excellence that lies within you!

Most of all to my amazing grandfather, Richard, who is a living, shining example of unconditional love, forgiveness and support. I love you.

And to all my friends and family who have supported me along the way.

CONTENTS

Chapter 1: Success
- *Explore. Dream. Discover* — 2
- *Going the Distance* — 4
- *Principles of Success* — 5
- *In Great Time* — 7
- *A Blessing in Disguise* — 7
- *Winning the Game* — 8
- *The Competitive Edge* — 10
- *Power of the Dream* — 12

Chapter 2: Walk By Faith
- *Mission to the Moon* — 17
- *God Blessed the Broken Road* — 20
- *Unanswered Prayers* — 21
- *Miracles* — 22
- *Well Done, My Good and Faithful Servant* — 25
- *Taking Bullets* — 25
- *The More You Seek, The More You Grow* — 27

Chapter 3: Power of Friendship
- *You Never Know* — 31
- *Put Yourself in Their Shoes* — 33
- *How to Treat Others* — 35
- *Don't Lead Others Astray* — 36
- *Restoring Friendships* — 38

Chapter 4: Vision to Reality
- *Go the Extra Mile* — 41
- *Vision to Reality* — 42
  - *Muhammad Yunas* — 43
  - *Florence Nightingale* — 44
  - *Robert Roth* — 47
  - *Nicholas Negroponte* — 48
- *The Entreprenuer* — 49

Chapter 5: Transparent Leaders
- *Transparent Leader* — 53
- *No "Butts"* — 54
- *Generation to Generation* — 54
- *Turn the Lights On* — 56
- *Accountability* — 57

Chapter 6: Time for Change
- *Change it Up* — 61
- *Root of All Evil* — 62
- *Unfinished Business* — 67
- *War* — 68
- *The Rock* — 69
- *One Door Closes, Another One Opens* — 71

Chapter 7: One Nation Under God
- *Our Future in Danger* — 76
- *Our Founding Fathers* — 77
- *Colors of the World* — 80
- *Millennium Development Goals* — 81

Chapter 8: The Bucket List
- *The Bucket List* — 86
- *Discovering Your Strengths* — 87
- *Power of Testimony* — 89
- *Making the Right Decision* — 90
- *Counseling* — 91
- *Charisma* — 92

Chapter 9: Walkin' On Holy Water
- *Listening When God Speaks* — 98
- *Place of Security* — 101
- *Big Fish* — 102
- *Blessings* — 103
- *Faith* — 104
- *Facing Giants* — 105

Key Words — 109

Life Quotes — 111
- *Life* — 111
- *Motivational* — 126
- *Faith* — 129
- *Friendship* — 131

Biblical Quotes — 133
- *Success* — 133
- *Goals, Visions, & Dreams* — 134
- *Awareness* — 135
- *Relationships* — 136
- *Choices* — 138
- *Faith* — 139

- *Crisis* — 141
- *Belief* — 142
- *Discipleship* — 143
- *Fundamentals* — 143
- *Training* — 145
- *Money* — 146
- *Performance* — 148
- *Giving Thanks* — 149
- *Game Plan* — 150
- *False Prophets* — 151
- *Heaven* — 151
- *Salvation* — 154

Author Bio Light At My Feet — 157
- *Past, Present, Future* — 157
- *Mission Statement* — 163

1 Success

"And now I will show you the most excellent way."

(1 Corinthians 12:31)

The biggest question throughout mankind has been, what is the purpose of life? The answer is simple. The purpose of life is living a life of purpose. Life is love, joy, sadness, pain, motivation, friendship, trust, integrity, progress, lessons, and faith. Life is everything we have experienced in the past, present, and will experience in the future. Life is trying things to see if they work. Life is lessons, which must be lived to be understood. Life is exactly what you do and do not put into it. A wasted life is an early death.

People are always searching for the ultimate pursuit of happiness. The purpose of this book is to inspire, encourage, and give hope to finding purpose and meaning in your life. It is important to look at the past, so we know where to go in the future.

In this book we will examine the basic principles in living a successful

Abraham Lincoln once said,

"In the end, it's not the years in your life that count. It's the life in your years."

and fulfilling life. We will discover how to properly *face giants* with diligence, integrity, honor, and grace. *Giants* are all the pain, struggles, and obstacles we endure in our journey of life. I will share stories spanning all areas of life, with the intent to help you find meaning and understanding.

I love the analogy of taking the good from the table and leaving the bad. In every person, in every situation, there is good that can be found. Through every experience and opportunity we can learn something. My hope in this book is that you will be shaken up a bit. These ideas should stir the heart and soul. It is extremely important to know what you believe and why. It is important to know your purpose! Otherwise, what is the purpose of our being and living here on this Earth?

EXPLORE. DREAM. DISCOVER

One of the greatest things in life is being able to learn from other people's mistakes. Also, being able to learn from other people's success. What are the basic characteristics of all successful people? I think you will discover they are all similar. First, successful people know what their purpose and direction is. If you don't know where you're headed, then you may not get there. Second, successful people have their priorities in the correct order. They put God first, then their family, then their friends.

Understand that successful people didn't make it all on their own. Somewhere along the line they had help getting there. All successful people had help from somebody along the way.

I myself have big aspirations of playing major league baseball someday. It has been a dream of mine since I was young. Every day I get up and check to see if I'm on a major league roster. If I'm not there, I get at it and go to work. The greatest things in life take much time and patience.

John Maxwell, Senior Pastor at Skyline Church, said,

"If you ever see a frog on a fence post, you know he had help getting there."

Nothing is easy, but it is the difficulty in things that make them great. If playing pro baseball was easy, everyone would be doing it. I believe this to be true. If you want something bad enough, then go after it full force. What's stopping you? Many doors will begin to open in your life when you work hard.

Don't be the one who regrets not following your dreams simply because you were too lazy and gave up. If you want to be a "nobody," then be a nobody. If you want to be a "winner," then be a winner. Make sure your "yes" is a yes, and your "no" is a no.

Thomas Jefferson wrote,

"The harder I work, the more luck I seem to have."

You can do anything you set your mind to. All you have to do, is know what you want, and go get it. Set a goal, then a deadline, and then go do it! Either do it, or don't do it. There is no try. I have

> *"Twenty years from now you will be more disappointed by the things you didn't do than by the ones you did do. So throw off the bowlines. Sail away from the safe harbor. Catch the trade winds in your sails. Explore. Dream. Discover."*
> *--Mark Twain*

found that opportunities tend to grow when they are seized.

GOING THE DISTANCE

One of the greatest success stories I've ever known is about a man named Daniel "Rudy" Ruettiger. I'm sure most people have seen the movie <u>Rudy</u>, but it contains a phenomenal message. Rudy came from a poor family and was told all his life what he could and couldn't do. His friends and even his family laughed at his hopes and dreams. Rudy was diagnosed with Dyslexia, a learning disability, as a child. Dyslexia primarily means having trouble with written language, especially reading and writing.

Time and time again he failed, but there was nothing that could stop him of his incredible dream of going to Notre Dame and playing football for the Irish. Rudy found a way to make it happen and do whatever it took. He worked harder than anyone, and opportunities soon began to multiply.

Rudy met people throughout his lifetime who helped him with his schooling and football training. He got himself into a junior college and found a tutor to help him boost his grades. Four years had passed by while working in a steel factory, then it took him another two years at Holy Cross Community College to finally get in to the university.

"It's not the size of the dog in the fight; it's the size of the fight in the dog."
--Mark Twain

The next goal was getting onto one of the top football teams in the nation. The biggest question is, "Are you willing to make sacrifices and do whatever it takes to fulfill your dreams?" Even though he wasn't the smartest guy, or even the biggest, Rudy found a way to be victorious.

PRINCIPLES OF SUCCESS

I believe there are seven main steps necessary to fulfill your dreams. I like using the term **P-U-R-P-O-S-E**.

Sir Winston Churchill once said,

- ❖ **P** – <u>P</u>ut your goals down on paper. *Whatever your goals are, write them down.*

"Never, never, never, quit."

- ❖ **U** – <u>U</u>tilize your time by getting your priorities in the right order. *Then put that list of goals on your*

"You got to be careful if you don't know where you're going, because you might not get there."
--Yogi Berra

desk, refrigerator, etc. Somewhere where you can see it easily every day as a reminder. This will help you stay focused and consistent.

- **R** – <u>Research.</u> *Do some research in finding out what is necessary to complete those goals. Talk to people, read, and study. Find out what it takes to be successful.*
- **P** – <u>Patience</u> *is key. Be sold out (some things have to be sacrificed). Sometimes this means missing out on trips and other fun things we would rather do instead. But know that some things have to be sacrificed to reach your goal. The prize is so much more rewarding when you know how much work you put toward achieving it. Know that every effort toward achieving your goal helps build character.*
- **O** – <u>Obstacles</u> *will always seem to find you on your journey. Remember that all the struggles in the road to success are minor compared to the ultimate goal. Don't get sidetracked with all the obstacles that come your way. There will always be hurtles, but continue straight ahead on your path to success. Let nothing phase or distract you. Always keep the bigger picture in mind.*
- **S** – <u>Sources.</u> *Use your resources. These can be trainers, tutors, mentors, accountability partners; basically anyone or anything that can help you achieve your goal.*
- **E** - <u>Excitement</u>. *You should always be excited and enthusiastic about fulfilling your dream. And lastly, PRAY! Pray and ask God to guide you and give you strength.*

IN GREAT TIME

Great things come in great time. Let's use the analogy of a sculptor and his work of art. One day a sculptor decides to carve an eagle out of a large piece of granite. At first he chizzles away and cuts out big chunks. However, it still doesn't look like much.

In fact, it doesn't look like anything yet except a big blob. But he chizzles and chizzles. Finally, he gets to a point where the rock begins to come to life. The formation of the wings, the head, and then the claws become reality. It takes a long time, but sooner or later all the features begin to form. The sculptor can finally see a light at the end of the tunnel. Once completed, it looks magnificent! It went from a big ugly rock to a perfectly shaped bald eagle.

Apply this analogy to your life. Work hard every single day and keep the bigger picture in mind. You may not see results right away. However, none of that work is wasted. Patience and persistence is key. Before you know it, you'll be there!

A BLESSING IN DISGUISE

Most people are afraid of change. Human beings like to remain in a place of comfort and security. But is change really a bad thing? Absolutely not! Life is all about change and making adjustments. Sometimes you have to roll with the punches and deal with giant obstacles.

For example, let's say that there are two sporting good stores in a small town. The two businesses are forced to compete and make certain changes. If one company carries more sporting goods and sells its products at a cheaper price, it will probably take business away from the other store. Thus, store number two will go out of business unless it makes changes. Possible changes may include: lowering their prices, adding more products, or lowering variable costs.

Whatever the solution, change is necessary! Sometimes change is a blessing in disguise. People often want different results in life, and yet they continue to do the same things day in and day out. If you want different results, you have to do different things!

Think about relationships for a second. Let's say that there is a situation where you can't seem to get along with a particular person. If you continue to do the same things and nothing changes, well, maybe it's time to change the way "you" think and act.

The solution to the problem is, *change yourself* first. As bad as we want to change others, people cannot change other people. They have to want to change themselves. I have come to realize that once you change yourself and focus on the positives in people, amazing things will begin to happen in your life, as well as the lives of others!

WINNING THE GAME

One of the biggest influences in my life was baseball coach Gary Adcock at California Baptist University. He taught us the importance of hard work and maintaining balance in life. Throughout the semester he taught us the importance of balancing not only our physical and mental side of the game, but our spiritual side as well. There was a good reason why we were one of the top teams in the nation!

Life Balance Chart

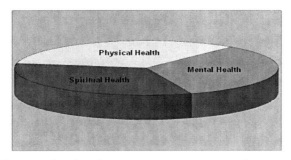

Let me be the first to invite you into the wonderful world of Coach Adcock. First, we would wake up at 3:15 a.m. to be ready to go down to the field by 4:00 a.m. for a little morning workout. I laugh when I say little because that is quite an understatement. From there we proceeded to run about three to four miles, depending on his mood. If his new-born baby kept him up all night, we ran even more.

Then at 5:45 a.m. we ran into the weight room. The morning workout would consist of ply-metrics, weight lifting, and cardio. After our morning workout we would attend class from 8:00 a.m. until 1:00 in the afternoon. Practice would start around 1:30 p.m., and we would play until dark.

Before each practice we were required to memorize a quote from the Bible or a particular word of the day. If any teammate skipped class, we just planned on running the entire weekend. This was by far the toughest thing I had ever done in my life. Every day was strenuous, exhausting, and required a lot of time and energy. Some days I felt as if I had nothing left and couldn't go on. I was in the hospital a total of six times throughout the semester due to health and stress related issues. My body was pushed to its furthest limit and taking quite a toll.

What was the significance of all this? Coach Adcock was trying to develop us into becoming good, strong, spiritual men. We didn't have time to goof off and go to parties. We didn't have time to get ourselves in trouble. It seemed like a lot at the time, which it definitely was, but it was necessary to become leaders. He wanted us to pay attention to detail and work hard for success. I have never seen a group of guys with as much motivation and integrity as I did at Cal Baptist.

Honestly, I felt that if I could survive this strenuous semester, I could accomplish anything. Coach uplifted his players and believed in them. That year we had four of our nine starters go on to play in the minors. That hard work and dedication was required to be the best. No other team in the state was running at 4:00 a.m. No other team was willing to sacrifice as much as we did. To be the best, you have to do what no one else is willing to do.

"Excellence is not a single act, but a habit. You are what you do repeatedly."
--Shaquille O'Neal

THE COMPETITIVE EDGE

Competition, if used in the right manner, can

be beneficial. Competition forces two people to be better. It causes them to work harder and strive to be the best. During Apollo 11, it required many of the greatest minds to compete to find a solution to get the three-man crew back to earth safely.

During the mission, the three crew members encountered massive damage to the space capsule. NASA put ten of the smartest people together in the boiler room. They were forced to put their minds together and find a solution. I love the statement, "Two heads are better than one." In this situation, that statement couldn't be more accurate.

There is only so much one person can do on their own. When you have a group of people, anything can be accomplished. One group member may know something that another does not. Someone else may have a better perspective on the situation. One person may have an idea which sparks another idea. Soon these ideas begin to perpetuate themselves. When everything is laid out on the table, you can begin to find the best possible solution.

Picture a sports team working to win the championship. During the season, all team members compete for the starting positions. Only the top players will start in the next game. Everyone is competing against the other, and soon everyone's skills begin to rapidly improve. Think about how much the team can achieve as a whole, when everyone is doing their best. The potential is endless, and the sky is the limit!

POWER OF THE DREAM

Having dreams is an important part of life. They are far more important than you can even imagine. Dreams help give meaning, purpose, and direction. They are also a wonderful gift from God. But what do we do when we are faced with giants on our journey? When you're going through struggles in life and you're at the bottom of the barrel, remember that the only place to go is up!

"Hold fast to your dreams, for if dreams die, life is a broken winged bird that cannot fly."
--Langston Hughes

Don't confuse slowing down with stopping. The biggest growth in life comes from getting out of your comfort zone. It's the building process that defines you. It is the process that builds your character. People are always watching you to see what you're going to do. If you tell someone you're going to be successful, trust me they're taking note of it. They may not tell you, but they're always watching.

Professional football player Tracey Easter once said,

"When you're in hell, don't get a motel."

Tracy said,

"When I started crying is when I started growing."

Sometimes it takes something drastic in life to get you going. Sometimes it takes something bad enough to get you off your hump and start fulfilling your dreams. The guilt of not pursuing your dreams will always outweigh the actual time you put toward achieving them. Champions are champions because they do the ordinary extraordinary. Be a complete person, strong in every area in life. "If there are holes in your ship, your gunna sink. Plug 'em up."

It is essential to learn how to turn *opposition* into *opportunity*. Sometimes, to do what we dream of doing, we have to do what we most dread to do. For example, if someone wants to be great leader, they need to have the *complete package*. Every area in life may be strong and well rounded, but there is always room for improvement. Quite possibly someone wants to be this "great leader," but struggles with speaking in front of large crowds. He or she has to get through the things they hate doing, to do what they love and dream of doing.

"Bullies" are the obstacles that try and keep you from achieving your dreams. Bullies can be anything from friends, accidents, physical handicaps, and even family; basically anyone or anything that stands in the way of your dreams. However, do not let anything distract you! The very fact that the "Bullies," (a.k.a. obstacles) are standing at your door means that you're already on your way toward greatness. Their opposition can actually be beneficial. These so called "Bullies" can help clarify and strengthen your resolve.

To illustrate, I was talking to someone about playing professional baseball one day in the future. The person's response was, "Why don't you just go out and get a real job! Why waste your time with something that isn't going to come true?" Many people would get upset, and it would hinder them from pursuing their dream.

For me, that statement only made my objective clearer than ever before. It confirmed what I wanted to do in the future all that much more! I took that criticism and used it as "Tacklin' Fuel" to work harder and get even more aggressive in my pursuit.

You and God are the only ones who need to be concerned about your dreams. If you want true success, take a look at these three steps:

> ➢ *Give your dream back to God. (Your dreams are given to you from Him. They are not yours to begin with!)*
> ➢ *Become cleansed, strengthened, and renewed through Him.*
> ➢ *God will give your dream back to you and more! And only then will you have perfect guidance and direction. With God you can accomplish anything!*

What do we do when we are faced with giants? What weapons do we have to go to battle for our dreams? Your weapons are every truth and lesson that you have learned along the way. The good news is that you are always ready for battle! This is exactly why we can't accomplish our dreams overnight. It is not about that instant gratification. If we have not completed our dreams, it is because the process is not yet finished. We are not yet ready to be living our dreams and placed in that position.

Success

Point to Remember: If you want something in life, then reach out and grab it!

Quote to Remember: "Never, never, never… quit."
--Sir Winston Churchill

Question to Consider: Are you willing to pay the price to fulfill your dreams?

PERSONAL APPLICATION:

1) Write down some of your goals for the next 5 – 10 years of your life.

   A) _____

   _____

   _____

   _____

   Deadline: _____

   B) _____

   _____

   _____

Facing Giants

_____

Deadline: _____

C)

_____

_____

Deadline: _____

D)

_____

_____

Deadline: _____

2 *Walk By Faith*

"Because you know that the testing of your faith develops perseverance. Perseverance must finish its work so that you may be mature and complete, not lacking anything."

(James 1:2-4)

MISSION TO THE MOON

There is a great story about a man who found happiness in his life by keeping the faith. His name was Charlie Duke. Charlie was an outstanding pilot for the U.S. Air Force. He served his country many years, then after that he joined NASA. His ultimate goal was to travel to the moon. Charlie soon had the opportunity to join Apollo 16 and go to that great big rock in the night sky. Apollo 16 was an eleven day journey to gain more insight about the surface of the moon and gather core samples. He said, "It was an opportunity of a lifetime."

Charlie had it all, many years serving his country, traveled to the moon, and even had a successful business for Anheuser Busch. Business was profitable, and yet there was still something missing in his life. Soon his family life began to fall apart. His wife and kids no longer respected him. His wife was struggling badly as well, and was even contemplating suicide. Charlie had always attended church growing up, but still didn't know who God was.

Then one day his wife attended a meeting at the local church. There was a panel of five guest speakers who spoke. She said, "I could see the glow on their faces. I could see that they truly knew God and were living a life filled with much joy and happiness." She wanted to have that same happiness in her life.

Every day she began to read her Bible and reach out to God. Neither Charlie nor his wife even knew how to pray, but they tried anyway. He said, "One day I could feel God's presence, and now I know beyond a shadow of a doubt that He is real."

About the time he became a believer, his father got sick and had to be hospitalized. Charlie didn't have a good relationship with his father, but was obviously concerned about his health and went to visit him. The doctor came to Charlie and told him that his father didn't have much longer to live. This made it extremely difficult for Charlie, especially because of the fact that his father had never even said that he loved him.

But he knew that God was with him and had His hand on the situation. One day Charlie walked into his father's room and asked if he could pray for him. His father said, "Yes, but I really don't think it will matter."

Charlie told his dad that he prayed that God would begin to take care of him and heal him. Then the Lord came to Charlie and said to just go and love your dad, and be by his side. He told his dad about this friend of his, and that every time he gets on an airplane he prays that angels will surround the plane during flight.

Then, one time after he prayed that prayer, they were flying along at 30,000 feet, and this one man looked out the window. God had allowed him to see an angel sitting on one of the wings. When he told his dad that story he just laughed and laughed.

His dad said, "I'll tell ya what. If I ever see an angel, he'd better have on a parachute."

Charlie said, "Well, dad, I pray you see an angel."

Charlie's brother, who was a doctor, even went to visit and told their father that God is love. His brother asked if he would receive Jesus into his heart, and then you will know peace from within. His father said he would, and then he accepted Jesus into his life. Even though he knew he was dying, once he prayed to receive Jesus, soon after a peace began to come over him.

It was as if a tidal wave of love splashed over him, washing away every bit of pain and sadness. The day Charlie's dad died, Charlie was obviously devastated, but knew that his dad was now with God. His father was no longer in pain or suffering. He just joined the party (heaven) early, as I like to call it.

The telephone rang that day and his wife said, "Call your friend Illea. He's got a word from God for ya." So he called his friend and his friend said, "Hey, I was praying for your dad today at 5:30 p.m. (which was the exact moment his dad had passed on), and God spoke to me when I was praying. God gave me a vision of two angels He was sending to collect your dad, to take

> *"In 1972, I rode Apollo 16 on a fantastic adventure. I used to say I could live for 10,000 years and never have an experience like walking on the moon. But the excitement and satisfaction of that walk doesn't compare with my walk with Jesus, a walk that lasts forever."*
>
> *--Charlie Duke*

him to heaven, and that he would die very soon."

God gave him a vision of two angels he was sending to collect your dad, to take him to heaven, and that he would die very soon." Then Illea said, "Charlie, the angels were very strange. They both had on big parachutes." Coincidence?

Charlie later said, "You can have that same love if you just open up your heart to God." It is by grace we have been saved through faith, and it's not of yourselves that is the gift of God, not by works so that no man can boast.

GOD BLESSED THE BROKEN ROAD

> *"Trust in the Lord with all your heart; and do not rely on your own understanding; think about Him in all your ways, and He will guide you on the right paths."*
>
> *--(Proverbs 3:5,6)*

Still haven't found the perfect person in your life? Still searching for your soul mate? Are you still depressed about a terrible break up with a guy or girl?

Do not worry! God is close to the broken hearted. He is planning that perfect person for you, so just "relax" for a little while. Be patient, and let God show you what will happen over time. If you're alone, make that "romance" and love for God while you're single. Spend that time, focus, and energy on Him.

Be a man or woman of integrity, and you will be a man or woman of strength! Trust in Him, and you will end up getting the one you've been longing for. Trust in God, for He is planning your life, your wife/husband, and everything else in the future. If you break up with a boyfriend or girlfriend and you're upset, you shouldn't be. You should be thanking God, because he/she wasn't right for you anyway, and it's time to move on.

UNANSWERED PRAYERS

Why does God answer some prayers and not others? Why doesn't He answer them right away? First, let me say this. God *does* answer prayers. All of them! But the answers will come in His time, not yours. Sometimes His answer will be a yes, sometimes a no, and sometimes it's wait. Whatever the answer, it is meant for your protection, even when you may not see it.

For example, my friend John prayed that his high school girlfriend would soon become his wife after graduation. He prayed that if God would grant this one request, He would never ask for anything again. A year or two after high school John and his girlfriend split up. They couldn't seem to get along and quickly grew apart.

> *"Faith is the substance of things hoped for, the evidence of things not seen."*
> *--(Hebrews 11:1)*

Years later John finally met a fantastic woman who eventually became his wife. As more time passed, John had a great marriage and two wonderful kids. One day while walking through the grocery store John saw his old high school sweetheart. But immediately he knew she was different from how she used to be. She wasn't the same as he had remembered. Then John looked over at his wife and kids and was thankful he hadn't married his high school girlfriend. His life was perfect, and he couldn't imagine it any other way.

The point I'm making is that God will answer you in His timing. He does this for our protection. Had God answered John's prayer of marrying his high school sweetheart, it could have been disastrous. Trust in the Man upstairs because He knows what He's doing.

Remember, God is outside the box and can see your whole life laid out before you even have any idea. Even though we can't see the future or what is going to happen to us, trust in Him. Let Him show you over time what His plans for your life are.

MIRACLES

When we are faced with an obstacle so great, sometimes the only thing we can do is pray for a miracle! But do miracles happen in the present day? Many people would argue that miracles happened thousands of years ago. But do they happen in the present? I would definitely say yes!

There are many examples, but let's focus on just two at the moment. The first example involves a police officer named Ben. It was a typical bright sunny day in San Diego, and Ben was patrolling Interstate 5 freeway. While his radar was on, he detected a car speeding and pulled the car over.

As he approached the driver's side of the vehicle, there was a man sitting in the driver's seat who looked suspicious. The driver quickly reached to his side and pulled out a gun. The man fired three shots at Ben. Luckily he was able to escape. Ben ducked, then moved to the front of the car, out of sight, yet clearly not out of harm's way. Ben kept his body below the car and fired rounds through the front windshield toward the driver. None of the shots hit, and the man continued to fire back.

All of a sudden the violence and chaos came to an end. The driver was hit in the shoulder and ceased fire. Ben was asked later what had happened. He said that he pulled the man over and then ducked to the ground when the man started shooting. Ben also said that he rapidly moved to the front of the car and began shooting from the front.

Ben didn't think that he had actually shot the man and was surprised that the gunshots had ended so abruptly. Now this is where the story gets interesting. When the driver was asked to retell the situation, he said that the police officer also ducked and moved to the front of the vehicle. But he said that the second officer had shot him.

Later Ben was asked if he was with his partner the day the event happened. Ben said, "No, my partner wasn't with me that day. He had gotten off early from work and was spending the day with his family." So who was that other officer who came to the rescue? Hmm…

The second story involves a girl who managed to survive in one of the most life-threatening situations you could ever imagine. This amazing story of survival was in the paper not long ago. This young girl lived with her mother who had just recently been divorced. Apparently, the ex-husband was still holding a grudge in the months following the divorce. The sick and twisted man killed the wife and buried both of them three feet underground. The little girl, age four, lay there right next to her dead mother several feet underground for three days!

An elderly man was walking his dog and heard noises from the ground. He knew someone or something was down there and needed help. Police, ambulances, and fire trucks came immediately. When they pulled the girl out, they were obviously astonished, but even more shocking, was the fact that she was completely unharmed.

They asked the little girl what happened and how she could have survived something like this. The girl said, "The man in white kept me safe. He was with me and protected me." Coincidence? Often times we expect miracles to be instantaneous, but sometimes they occur over a period of years and aren't as easy to recognize.

WELL DONE, MY GOOD AND FAITHFUL SERVANT

What will God say to you when you finally reach the pearly gates in Heaven? Well done, my good and faithful servant? I sure want Him to say that to me when I pass on. This is a huge wake-up call for many of us. One of the biggest requests from God is getting as many people to Heaven as possible. He loves all his children and wants them all to be with Him in Heaven.

Rick Warren, Senior Pastor of Saddleback Church, wrote, "Is anyone going to be in heaven because of you? Will anyone in heaven be able to say to you, I want to thank you? I'm here because you cared enough to share the good news with me. Imagine the joy of greeting people in heaven whom you helped get there. Only people are going to last forever."

> *"The eternal salvation of a single soul is more important than anything else you will ever achieve in life."*
> *--Rick Warren*

TAKING BULLETS

Avoid impatience and be purified by the process. Avoid complaining and say "thank you" to God. You

> *"Many are the plans in a man's heart, but it is the Lord's purpose that prevails."*
> *--(Proverbs 19:21)*

should be thanking God to even be having the problems we encounter in life. There is absolutely no way to learn how to get through a problem if we never experience one. We experience things in life to share the lessons we've learned with others. If you have gone through something tragic in life, use that to help others who are going through the same situation.

When we endure trials and tribulations, we are simply being tested. God knows what will happen to us in the end, but wants to see how we handle these stressful situations. He wants to see our character. Are we going to handle situations as Jesus would? Or are we going to handle challenges selfishly and on our own terms?

When you have God in your life, you can take bullets. God has gotten us through everything up to this point. Why wouldn't He get us through the rest of our lives safely? Think of the movie <u>Scarface</u>. In the last scene of the movie Tony Montana takes on twenty men by himself. He is shot numerous times in the chest, but remains standing. He remains strong and powerful even though he is taking on lots of bullets.

> *"Your word is a lamp to my feet and a light for my path."*
> *--(Psalm 119:105)*

The point is, we will be able to take bullets when we have God on our side. We will be strong enough to get through any challenges life throws our way.

And we will do it without fear, because we have the most powerful force in the world on our side!

THE MORE YOU SEEK, THE MORE YOU GROW

The more I seek God, the more I learn, grow, and get to know Him. Every time I go to church, see a guest speaker, listen to others, I have an opportunity to learn and grow. Every experience (surgery, break-up, etc.) has gotten me closer and closer to God. God knows what He is doing. Talk to people, find out what they know, gain knowledge, and broaden your education.

Be patient. God's timing is perfect. Good things will come if you just remain faithful. Life is hard enough, so always think positively and focus on the things that are going well. You will find you become much happier when you have a positive outlook on life. Through every trial you either become closer to God or further away. It's a lot better going through life with God than without Him. It not only affects your life here on earth, but your life in eternity as well!

God is shaping and molding you every single day. Make time to spend with Him. He has helped me make it through the thick and the thin. Always! When you're down, depressed, and feeling helpless, simply focus, pray, and worship Him. Take the focus off all negative and let Him show you His grace and love. Spend more time praising Him than focusing on all the "bull" in your life.

God is a rock. He is solid and never changing. People are only human and will eventually let you down. People tend to change, and aren't always stable. But

God is never changing. He will never let you down. God will never be unaccountable, lie, cheat, steal, or cause you harm. So who are you going to put your trust in?

Focus on what you need to be doing, and be a soldier for God. Go to war, but the right kind of war. Spiritual war! It's a battle to save souls! Be open to what God is teaching you. As I grow older, I learn more, love more, feel more, and can give more! I'm always reminded of my purpose when I spend time with God. He always helps redirect and guide me when I talk to Him.

> *"Teach us to number our days carefully so that we may develop wisdom in our hearts."*
> *--(Psalm 90:12)*

The only way you're going to learn is to go out and seek answers for yourself, through reading, searching, and talking to others. If you're trying to figure out the solution to something, don't just sit back and do nothing. Go out and do what is necessary to find the answer. Read the Bible slowly. Let it sink in, understand it, and God will speak to you. See what He shows you through reading His word.

Walk by Faith

Point to Remember: The more you seek, the more you grow!

Quote to Remember: "Your word is a lamp to my feet and a light for my path."
(Psalm 119:105)

Question to Consider: How can I remind myself each day that life is really about living for God, and not about me?

PERSONAL APPLICATION:

Write down some things you need to pray about, and later see how God answered those prayers.

PRAYERS:

A)
_____
_____

_____
_____

Date: _____

B)

_____
_____

_____
_____

Date: _____

C)

_____
_____

_____
_____

Date: _____

D)

_____
_____

_____
_____

Date: _____

3 *Power of Friendship*

"A gentle answer turns away wrath, but a harsh word stirs up anger."

(Proverbs 15:1)

YOU NEVER KNOW

Believing the best in people usually brings the best out of people. Friendship and building relationships with others is extremely important. Humans are designed to live in communities, not to live alone. A great example of the power of friendship involves a boy named Greg.

"Only a life lived for others, is a life worthwhile."
--Albert Einstein

Greg lived in a small town in Indiana, and many considered him to be kind of an outsider. He had no friends at school and struggled deeply in his family life. He was picked on a lot in class and didn't know how to cope with all these issues.

Martin Luther King Jr. once said,

"In the end, we will remember not the words of our enemies, but the silence of our friends."

Then one day a guy came up and asked how he was doing. He said, "It looks like you could use a friend." After school the guy asked if he could walk back to his house with him because he lived nearby. The boy was new at the school and was also trying to make new friends. They ended up spending the rest of the day together, just hanging out and having fun.

Little did the guy know, but Greg was planning on committing suicide that very day. Greg had kept a gun in his locker and was planning to end his life right after class. But because somebody else reached out and befriended him, it literally saved his life! The two became the best of friends and went on to do great things in life.

That story is so powerful because it just goes to show that a little extra effort and reaching out can change a life. So speak up and do something about it. If you see someone struggling, no matter who it is, friend, stranger, whoever, go talk to them. Help them in any way possible because you don't know what they might be going through.

"The true measure of a man is how he treats someone who can do him absolutely no good."

--Samuel Johnson

PUT YOURSELF IN THEIR SHOES

I myself experienced an interesting situation with a bad roommate in college. Jeremy always seemed to be angry and depressed. He had a lot of trouble getting along with others and dealing with the issues in his life. Jeremy was constantly getting into fights and continually running into trouble with the law. I didn't know what I had gotten myself into when I asked him to be my roommate. I figured we both played ball together, so he was probably a pretty good guy.

Soon I ran into all kinds of problems with Jeremy. There were issues with him not paying rent, bringing all kinds of drugs into the apartment, and trashing the place every weekend. This was just the tip of the iceberg. We began to fight all the time and soon began to hate one another. I couldn't seem to figure out why we couldn't get along. I mean, I thought I was a pretty reasonable guy and was a lot of fun to be around.

The problems only magnified and got much worse from there. I tried talking to Jeremy about moving out because this situation just wasn't working. It then escalated into him talking about pulling a gun on me. Now, along with everything, I was in fear of my life being in danger! He already had a bad track record. He had been thrown in jail for stealing and charged with assault and battery.

I did everything I could to make the situation better. Finally, one day I took a much softer approach. I sat down with him and asked what was going on in his life. "Is there anything I can do to make this relationship better?" To my surprise he actually opened up and talked to me about all the struggles he had been through. Jeremy began to tell me that he lived in a rough neighborhood and had nobody in his life he could talk to. His mother and father were both drug addicts and were never around when he was growing up. The only influences in his life were drugs, violence, and the local gangs in the town.

He told me one particular story that absolutely blew me away. One day, he and his friend had ordered a pizza. When his friend went to pay the pizza guy at the front door, there was a man standing there holding a gun to his head. Jeremy had walked around the corner to see what all the commotion was about, and right then, the man shot his friend once in the head and three times in the chest.

The gunman killed him over a $100 debt, which had not yet been paid back. As you can imagine I was shocked when I heard this story. Suddenly, I gained a whole new perspective on the situation and realized why he acted the way he did. I was able to step outside the box for a moment.

I, on the other hand, grew up in a good neighborhood and had never experienced anything close to what my roommate had been through. Sometimes we have to put ourselves in other people's shoes to understand what is going on in their minds. Prior to knowing what he had witnessed, I simply could not understand why he was so angry. I'm so glad I took the time and effort to talk to him, because after that we became good friends. I was able to help him with some of his issues and help get him back on his feet. I learned a lot from that experience.

The biggest thing I can say is, do not judge others. If someone attacks you, it's probably because there is a deeper issue beneath the surface. It may be an issue or problem that you don't know anything about. So be there for them and help them in any way possible.

Later, I asked myself, "What good could possibly come of this situation?" Well, once I got to know Jeremy a little better, I found out that he was a personal trainer. It couldn't have come at a better time because I was preparing to try out for an independent baseball team and desperately needed to get in shape.

I helped my roommate, and he in turn helped me. You get out of life exactly what you put into it. If you put negative things into your life, you'll obviously get negative out of life. However, if you only put positive things into your life, well, then positive things are going to come out! The choice is really up to you.

HOW TO TREAT OTHERS

Dale Carnegie wrote about a relationship between a boss and an employee. One day the boss was walking by and saw that three employees were messing around in the break room far too long.

Instead of yelling at them and telling them to get back to work immediately, he stopped,

"The tongue has the power of life and death, and those who love it will eat its fruit."
--(Proverbs 18:21)

walked up to them, and joined in on their conversation. He grabbed a soda and began laughing and joking with them. He befriended them first and got to know them on a personal level.

Once this was set in place, he nicely asked if they could go back to work. The boss took a much gentler approach instead of tearing their heads off. This approach is more effective because people do not respond well to being yelled at and feeling unappreciated. On top of all that, the boss made a whole group of new friends.

The moral is that everyone is important and deserves to be treated with respect.. Because the boss was the type of person whom he was, the company began to grow immensely. He gave employees more say in the company, and they began to feel like they were a part of the team. When you do this in business, relationships, etc., you will notice tremendous growth and longevity. People will begin to enjoy coming in to work because it is a wonderful atmosphere, and they feel like they are important.

DON'T LEAD OTHERS ASTRAY

"Be nice to people on your way up because you will meet them on your way down."
--Jimmy Durante

People struggle with life enough, and it is important that you don't push them further away from where they are supposed to be. For example, don't be an accomplice to someone who has a drinking problem or is underage. If you are friends with someone who has a problem with alcohol and you are always inviting them to parties where there will be drinking, what do you think is going to happen? You're simply putting even more temptation in front of them. How hard do you think it will be for them then?

There was a boy in San Diego who just recently died in a car crash, along with three of his friends. The four boys were all in high school and wanted to attend a big party over the weekend. They figured that they needed to get a whole bunch of alcohol for the party to be cool and fit in. One of the boys asked his older brother, who was twenty-one, if he would buy them alcohol. The brother agreed and bought them drinks for the party. The young boys went to the top of the hill before the party and started drinking. All of the boys were drinking, including the driver.

About a minute from getting to the house, the driver lost control of the vehicle and the car went crashing down into a valley. All of the boys lost their lives. Who was responsible for all this? Well, all of them were responsible, especially the older brother. Because of one bad decision, four people lost their lives. It not only affected their lives, but the lives of their families as well. Just imagine how that older brother felt for what he had done. Don't be an accomplice!

"The mouth of the righteous is a fountain of life."
--(Proverbs 10:11)

RESTORING FRIENDSHIPS

The Bible says, as a faithful donkey, you will speak the unspoken. Take the time to restore broken relationships. It will not only change your life, but theirs as well. God wants to walk with us. He put us here on Earth for Him. Wherever you are, you will be there to carry out God's work. God will be there to resolve issues in people's lives by using *you*!

If you see someone who is sad or depressed, go up and talk to them. Find out how they're doing and if there is anything you can do to help. Even if you don't know what to say to that person, don't let this stop you. When you're walking with God, a funny thing happens; He will be able to speak through you! While you are on your way to talk to the person, suddenly words begin to culminate in your mind. He will give the right words to say and guide you in the right direction.

However, it is only when you make the effort to do what is right when He will bless you. Let God use you as a light and as mirror image of Him. When people look at you, do they see God? He speaks to us in many ways, but one of the biggest is

Rick Warren once said,

"Relationships are always worth restoring. Because life is all about learning how to love, God wants us to value relationships and make the effort to maintain them instead of discarding them whenever there is a rift, a hurt, or a conflict."

through other people. When a pastor is trying to write a sermon and runs out of things to say, God speaks. He gives him the knowledge and wisdom to share to His people. When someone helps somebody else in a time of need, this is God's work carried out through others. Are you letting God use you? Are you a light to others?

Jesus said, "God blesses those who work for peace, for they will be called the children of God."

Peacemaking does not mean to avoid conflict. It is not running from a problem or pretending it doesn't exist. Being afraid to resolve a conflict is actually cowardice. According to Rick, we restore broken relationships by, talking to God before talking to someone. Always take the initiative. Sympathize with their feelings. Confess your part of the conflict. Attack the problem, not the person. Cooperate as much as possible. And finally, emphasize reconciliation, not resolution.

Power of Friendship

Point to Remember: Life is all about building healthy relationships.

Quote to Remember: "Only a life lived for others, is a life worthwhile." --Albert Einstein

Question to Consider: Do others see God when they look at you?

PERSONAL APPLICATION:

Write down some things that you need to improve on in relationships and dealing with people.

A)

B)

C)

D)

4 *Vision to Reality*

"Delight yourself in the Lord and He will give you the desires of your heart."

(Psalms 37:4)

GO THE EXTRA MILE

How do we attempt to change the world? What impact can I make? There's a man named Mel Young who is a social entrepreneur who is helping change this world.

Mel was walking around one day and saw there were far too many homeless people just on this one particular street. He asked, "What can I do to get them off the streets?" Soon after, he came up with an idea for having a Homeless World Cup. His vision was to get the homeless off the streets and onto various soccer teams throughout the world. Mel and his crew

"An individual has not started living until he can rise above the narrow confines of his individualistic concerns to the broader concerns of all humanity."
-Martin Luther King, Jr.

would go up to the homeless and ask if they would like to try out and join the training program to play soccer and represent their country.

The training program lasts a couple of months, and if they are good enough, they get to play in the Homeless World Cup which is held once a year. Even if some don't make the team, it doesn't matter. Because in the process of training, they get in shape, get off drugs, and now can go out and find jobs. Players who made the teams can put on their resumes that they got to represent their country. Psychological problems also begin to decline because they are now a part of a team and build lasting friendships.

Currently, 17,000 players joined the training program in Denmark alone in 2007. There are 48 countries and 500 players, competing for the next Homeless World Cup in 2008. Amazingly, the numbers continue to increase. The Homeless World Cup has had a 77% success rate for getting homeless off the streets. You will not see any other business with this high success rate anywhere in the world!

The event is sponsored by local and international sponsors, like Nike and Gatorade. This is so amazing because it all stemmed from just one man's idea. He wanted to do something to better this world, and he did just that. Just imagine if everyone on this earth did something.

"It's kind of fun to do the impossible."
--Walt Disney

VISION TO REALITY

Many people don't pay enough attention to social

entrepreneurs. But these are people who are helping change the world we live in. These are people who have the desire and passion to help others.

Africa is one of the poorest countries in the world. Ninety-five percent of the population is living on less than a dollar a day.

"Dreams pass into the reality of action. From the actions stems the dream again; and this interdependence produces the highest form of living."
--Anais Nin

About half of the world's poor are suffering from water-related diseases. Over 6,000 people, mainly children, die each day by consuming unsafe drinking water. Today, 1.1 billion people are without access to safe drinking water. A company called LifeStraw came up with an invention that purifies surface water into safe drinking water. LifeStraw offers relief from waterborne diseases of major public concern such as typhoid, cholera, dysentery and diarrhea. This invention has allowed people to drink clean, fresh water wherever they go.

MUHAMMAD YUNAS

Muhammad Yunas is another example of someone who is helping change the world. Yunas has had great success helping people get out of poverty. In Bangladesh, he has found a way to provide people with credit without requiring collateral. Yunas developed a revolutionary micro-credit system called the Grameen Bank.

This bank is cost effective and a powerful weapon to fight poverty. PBS did a report on Yunus which said:

"We tried to ignore it," he says. "But then skeleton-like people began showing up in the capital, Dhaka. Soon the trickle became a flood. Hungry people were everywhere. Often they sat so still that one could not be sure whether they were alive or dead. They all looked alike, men, women, and children. Old people looked like children, and children looked like old people."

"Nothing in the economic theories I taught reflected the life around me. How could I go on telling my students make believe stories in the name of economics? I needed to run away from these theories and from my textbooks and discover the real-life economics of a poor person's existence."

When Yunus went to the nearby village of Jobra, he learned the true economic realities of the poor. He desperately wanted to help. Yunas was able to come up with several plans while working with his students. He soon discovered that one of his many ideas was more successful than the rest, offering people tiny loans for self-employment. The Grameen Bank was born, and an economic revolution had begun.

FLORENCE NIGHTINGALE

Probably one of the greatest examples of someone who cares for others is Florence Nightingale. Nightingale was also known as the "Lady of the Lamp." She was born in Victorian England into a wealthy family. Seeking work for a woman of wealth in England was

Facing Giants

unheard of, especially one looking for work in the nursing field.

Her father got word of this and banned her from studying and spending time on nursing. Privately and discreetly she studied the history of hospitals and convalescent homes. Even when a man asked for her hand in marriage, she declined because she knew her purpose was to focus on nursing. Nightingale's entire life was devoted to helping and improving the lives of others.

In 1853, at age thirty-three, Nightingale was finally allowed to receive an unpaid position as superintendent of the Institution for the Care of Sick Gentlewomen in London. From there, she had gained a reputation as an excellent administrator. "Then, in the fall of 1854, English soldiers were dispatched to Crimea, on the north coast of the Black Sea, to fight alongside Turkish forces at war with Russia. Through the advent of war journalism, the English public began receiving reports about wounded soldiers in the Crimean campaign being left to die without basic medical attention." --David Bornstein

There were over 2,400 sick and wounded soldiers in the barracks and general hospitals. Spanning up to four miles long, soldiers lay in filthy clothes and cots. Immediately, Nightingale set out to find a solution and a cure for what was causing such a high death toll. Nightingale had a combination of tack, good sense, political influence and calm authority.

She was the first to introduce meticulous record-keeping, made sure that soldiers ate with sterilized cutlery, and wore freshly cleaned clothes. Nightingale helped construct new kitchens and laundry rooms, and also made sure that soldiers washed with fresh towels and soap. She would always give a little extra effort and make nightly rounds to comfort patients. "She established reading rooms, recreation rooms, classes and lectures, and even got soldiers to send remittances home, a feat the army had deemed impossible." --David Bornstein

Florence Nightingale was a pioneer in the use of graphical tools (such as polar-area or 'pie' charts). She employed these charts to stress the need for change. She was forced to go to great lengths to get her point across and produce change among hospitals. Nightingale even presented her material to officials in the army medical department and War Office. In 1859 she published the first edition of "Notes on Hospitals." These notes would later go on to revolutionize the theory of hospital construction and layout. She established the Nightingale Training School for Nurses, in 1860. This was intended to provide nurses with proper instruction and training, and providing them with housing.

Florence Nightingale was single-handedly responsible for turning nursing into a modern, respectable profession. During her life, she wrote an estimated 12,000 letters and 200 books. She also wrote and created hundreds of reports and monographs as well. Talk about a huge desire to help others! She took the time and devoted her life to helping people, and look at the impact she made! What difference are you making?

ROBERT ROTH

"The official unemployment rate among 15-24 year olds in Switzerland is 5.4%. However, the estimated number of unregistered, unemployed youth is around 20,000. If this is taken into account, the youth unemployment rate is 9%. Youth unemployment is particularly tragic, since the young people in question will have little chance of finding employment later on if they are unable to acquire the necessary qualifications at this stage. Most end up receiving social welfare benefits.

Job Factory has calculated that each unemployed youth costs the government around Sfr. 60,000 (about US $47,000) per year. For the city of Basle alone, this is a total of Sfr. 120 million (about US $94 million) per year for 2,000 unemployed." --Schwab Foundation

Robert Roth won the Social Entrepreneur award in 2005, and found a solution to this problem. Roth founded the Job Factory which offers a second chance in the job market for teenagers and young adults. By the age of 23 he was in charge of a retail store. In 1976 he founded Weizenkorn, which is the largest employer of young people with psychological problems in Switzerland. He soon began to notice that more and more young people, not just with those problems, couldn't seem to find jobs and were losing hope. This encouraged him to find a solution to this problem.

In 1999 he conceived the idea for the Job Factory, then it was launched a year later. The Job Factory gives teenagers and young adults a fresh start into the job market. The goal is to keep kids off the welfare program, which typically end their careers before they have even started. The Job Factory offers a wide range of internship opportunities including: management, technical support, mechanic, building guitars, etc. The internships typically last for about six months in more than fifteen different professions.

NICHOLAS NEGROPONTE

Nearly two billion children in third world countries are inadequately educated or receive any education at all. Less than one third of these children do not even complete the fifth grade. This issue goes even deeper than what meets the eye. Just like their parents, these children are consigned to poverty and isolation. It is a vicious cycle, and many of them will never know what the light of learning could mean in their lives. Their governments struggle as well to compete in a rapidly evolving economy. Often they lack the finances and resources to do so.

So what is one way we can help these children broaden their education without it being too expensive? Nicholas Negroponte came up with a solution. Negroponte and OLPC (non-profit organization) developed the $100 laptop. This is a simplified computer called XO, which provides Internet access and many other educational tools at a cheap cost.

> *"To live is the rarest thing in the world. Most people exist, that is all."*
> *--Oscar Wilde*

"The computer -uniquely fosters 'learning' by allowing children to "think about thinking", in ways that are otherwise impossible. Using the XO as both their window on the world, as well as a highly programmable tool for exploring it, children in emerging nations will be opened to both illimitable knowledge and to their own creative and problem-solving potential."

"The best way to predict the future is to invent it."
--Alan Kay

THE ENTREPRENUER

All of us have the resources and abilities to fulfill our dreams. For instance, there were two guys living in an apartment above a pizzeria in Santa Monica. While watching some funny videos of their friends one day they had an idea to put their funny videos, and allow others to post videos, on the Internet.

These were the same two guys who developed YouTube. YouTube just sold for millions and millions of dollars. Simple idea, right? Well, it was. The point I'm trying to make is if you have a good idea or goal you would like to achieve, then go out and accomplish it. There is nothing holding you back!

One day a man was walking down the street and saw that the neighbors were having a garage sale. An idea popped into

"The average person thinks he isn't."
--Father Larry Lorenzoni

his head to have a garage sale, but put it online. This idea turned into eBay. He took a simple idea, (allowing people to buy and sell online) and turned it into reality.

A young man named Tom Anderson had an idea for a website. The idea was to allow people to have their own web page and communicate with one another. I think you might know the site; it's called MySpace. MySpace just sold for 68 million dollars to Rupert Murdoch, founder of the Fox Network. Tom took a good idea and ran with it.

Someone had to come up with the idea for the toothbrush. Someone else came up with the idea for a straw. Somebody else came up with the idea for email. These are basic and practical things that people use every day. What I'm trying to get across is that if you have a good idea, run with it. Turn that idea into reality. Create an invention that helps with daily living. Come up with an idea that makes something easier.

Use your abilities and God given talents to help others. There are so many things in this world that have yet to be invented or discovered. With all the technology and resources readily available to us, use them. There's no excuse not to do something great!

John F. Kennedy was asked the definition of "happiness." He responded, "The full use of your powers along lines of excellence."

> ## Vision 2 Reality
>
> **Point to Remember:** The future is exactly what you make it!
>
> **Quote to Remember:** "It's kind of fun to do the impossible." --Walt Disney
>
> **Question to Consider:** How can I make a difference?

PERSONAL APPLICATION:

Write down any ideas, inventions, visions you would like to accomplish within the next 3-5 years.

A) _____
_____

_____
_____

Date: _____

B)

Date: _____

C)

Date: _____

D)

Date: _____

5 Transparent Leaders

"For out of the outflow of the heart the mouth speaks."

(Matthew 12:34)

TRANSPARENT LEADER

People can see right through you. They can determine whether you're a man or woman of honesty and integrity. Or they can see if you're a fake. Are you being a transparent leader? Can others see the light of God through you? I will use the Diamond analogy to illustrate my point. When you look at a diamond, and there is no light in the room, you see nothing. The diamond does not sparkle or shine bright.

However, when there is light in the room, the light hits the diamond, and it shines brighter than ever. The point is, we need the light of God to shine. Imagine as if we are the diamond, God provides the light (His love), and then we become magnificent!

NO "BUTTS"

As Pastor Miles McPherson would say, "Don't let your 'buts' keep you from getting into heaven. I would help this person 'but, or I would be faithful 'but.' Don't let your 'buts' get in the way of God's purpose. There is a good reason your 'butt' is in the back!" God can use anyone for His purpose.

In the Bible, God took Abraham even at his old age, and he built a nation. Joseph was sold into slavery and was eventually made a ruler. Moses had a bad temper and even killed a man, but walked with God and delivered Israel from Egypt. David was an adulterer and murderer as well, but repented, was forgiven, and still used by God. The list goes on and on with people who have committed the most terrible sins, and yet still be used for God's glory. There are no excuses not to do "good." No "butts!"

GENERATION TO GENERATION

What causes people to stumble? What turns a good and innocent child toward depression and low self-esteem as an adult? Granted, as an adult, you can choose who you want to be. You have the option to make certain choices and have your own set of morals and values. But does a parent have a large impact on the child's life when that child becomes an adult? The answer is a big yes! Family environment has almost everything to do with determining how a child turns out when reaching adulthood. Let me give you an example.

I have a friend who grew up in an abusive family environment. His father treated him as if he didn't exist. My friend hardly ever got to spend any time with his father, especially any quality time. The only time he ever got to see his dad was at ten o'clock at night when he was pissed off and upset with work. His father would beat him both verbally and physically.

My friend hated his father throughout most of his young life. As soon as he graduated, he moved as far away from his so called "home" as possible. My friend didn't speak to his father for twelve years! Not a phone call, postcard, birthday card, nothing!

My friend just recently got married to a beautiful girl from California. More good news is that they also just recently had a baby girl. However, my friend still wasn't speaking to his father. Two more years had passed, and his wife still had never had a chance to meet his father. Even more concerning was the fact that his father had never met the wife nor his beautiful granddaughter. My friend had everything in the world going for him, except one important ingredient -- his father's love. Because of his father's actions it affected him most of his life.

My friend struggled with depression, self-esteem, and self-worth. The depression soon led to unhappiness and later adultery. So my question is, "Where does it all end?" How many times does one negative generation have to affect the generations that follow?

In my experience I have seen how people can be greatly affected by their family environment. I deeply encourage you to not make the same mistakes. Plant

> *"Wise men make proverbs, but fools repeat them."*
> *–Samuel Palmer*

only good seeds among the young because they will be running this country when you are old and grey!

TURN THE LIGHTS ON

I'm sure everyone loves that feeling of life, spirit, and that sense of being truly alive! I always feel this way when I am on board with God. When I'm praising, worshiping, and giving it all to Him. Take the time to look at God's creation (nature, animals, people, etc.). These things are beautiful and will help you realize God is good, and He is up there. Just because everyone else is lying, stealing, and cheating, don't stoop to their level.

Be a light; one where people can come to you and ask you for help and guidance. And then point them straight to God. Focus on the blessings in your life. Understand that God has set you free to be different. When someone is cruel toward you, then you have the freedom to stop and pray for them. Be different from everyone else and become the miracle. You don't have to act just like them.

> *"There are only two ways to live your life. One is as though nothing is a miracle. The other is as though everything is a miracle."*
> *--Albert Einstein*

Keep in mind that as soon as you make the decision to walk with God, many *obstacles* will begin to come your way. There are always going to be trials and tribulations in life. That is life! However, it doesn't mean you

"God didn't promise us smooth sailing, but He did promise us a safe landing."

shouldn't try. God is simply testing you to see how you will handle the situation. If you are faithful, He will bless you!

Until the day you die, there is always going to be someone telling you that you can or can't do something. Don't let others poison you. Get the negative people out of your life! Surround yourself with people who are going to keep you on track and on the righteous path.

ACCOUNTABILITY

With all the struggles we have to endure in life, sometimes it is necessary to get help. We cannot make it through everything on our own. If you are struggling with a certain problem on a consistent basis and can't shake it, don't worry. Find someone who can help keep you accountable and stay on the right track. For example, if you struggle with pornography, tell someone. I know it is difficult to put ourselves out there and reveal our deepest secrets. It is tough to show others that we are slip-

As Mrs. Doubtfire would say,

"Help is on the way, dear!"

ping because we always want others to only see our best.

The most important thing we can do is fix the problems in our lives. If you struggle with something, tell a friend, then have that friend ask you every single day if you are staying on track. Ask them to ask you whatever it is you struggle with the most. Trust me, you know there are things in your life that need changing. It's time to get those skeletons out of the closet!

When you begin to resolve these issues, you will notice wonderful things begin to happen in your life. One bad area in your life can affect all other areas. I'm sure you've heard the saying, "One bad apple can ruin the whole barrel."

For instance, if you're generally not a liar, but you tell someone a lie, then you will have to tell another lie just to cover up the first. The lying soon becomes a trend and will come back around to haunt you. It can become a repetitive threat and soon destroy you from the inside out.

Let's get back to our first example, the struggle with pornography. At first it seems harmless. You may currently have good morals and views about women. Unfortunately, this will begin to diminish over time. It is a slow process, but when you're looking at these pictures, your views begin to change.

You start looking at women as objects instead of your sisters in Christ. You start lusting after every good looking woman you see. This may later cause you to cheat on your wife or future wife one day. It is the start of the end! If you see a problem in your life, nip it in the bud as soon as possible. Don't let temptation destroy you!

Transparent Leaders

Point to Remember: Don't let your "buts" keep you from getting to heaven.

Quote to Remember: "There are only two ways to live your life. One is as though nothing is a miracle. The other is as though everything is a miracle."
--Albert Einstein

Question to Consider: Are there things in my life that I need to get rid of?

PERSONAL APPLICATION:

Write down any area that needs improvement in your family life. How can you make life better within your home?

A) _____
_____
_____

B) _____
_____
_____

C)

D)

6 Time for Change

"For I know the plans I have for you,' declares the Lord, 'plans to prosper you and not to harm you, plans to give you hope and a future."

(Jeremiah 29:11)

CHANGE IT UP

Most people set goals in their lifetime, either to be a musician, famous actor or actress, or even a professional athlete. But are they going to do whatever it takes to get there?

Are they willing to pay the ultimate price? Are they willing to sacrifice everything to get there? Many people get frustrated when they want to fulfill their dreams and never get there. Even worse, people can even become depressed, struggle with self-esteem issues, and do nothing positive with their lives. To reiterate, if you want something you've never had, then you have to do something you've never done!

Example, let's say you are trying to get into great shape, but can't seem to

"You miss 100% of the shots you don't take."
--Wayne Gretzky

> *"Your whole outlook on life revolves around what you put in your body."*
> *--Taylor Kitsch*

make it happen. First, let's examine the facts. You may be consistent and go to the gym every single day, but for some reason you still don't notice any changes. Something else might have to be changed first to achieve success. Maybe you're not eating the right foods. Or quite possibly you are not exercising the proper mechanics.

If you want to achieve your goals, you need to find out exactly what is required, then do it. And do it on a *consistent basis*! If there's a day you're tired and stressed out from work, it doesn't matter. Go to the gym! In all reality you'll find that once you get to the gym, your second wind comes anyway. And then once you're done, you feel fantastic. One of the best ways to overcome stress is by exercising! Both physical and mental health goes hand in hand.

Whatever you put in your body is exactly what you're going to get out of it. It's okay if you slip up every now and then. Just start right up again and get back on board.

> *"I have not failed. I've just found 10,000 ways that won't work."*
> *–Thomas Alva Edison*

ROOT OF ALL EVIL

Money is not the root of all evil. The *love* of money is! It is quite obvious that you can have all the money in the world, but if you don't have anyone to share it with, it's useless. Money can be dangerous if you're not smart. Think of a ten-year-old boy on Christmas morning. He gets a new toy and feels like he is on top of the world! Then a couple of days later that toy is in the back of the closet, no longer to be played with again.

Margaret Fuller once said,

"Men, for the sake of making a living, forget to live."

Adults are the same way if consumed by money. First it's a new outfit, then a new car, then a new house. *Each time having to one up the other*. It's a dangerous road to travel, and is never fulfilling or satisfying in the long run. It's only a temporary fix. It is important to make sure that your priorities are in the correct order. What are you doing with your money? Are you spending it wisely? Are you spending it on others and on God?

Ask yourself these questions and be honest with yourself.

Let's take a close look at Hollywood, for instance. Many actors, actresses, musicians, and famous athletes have it all. Right? Well, they have a lot of money, that's for

"Honor the Lord with your wealth, with the first fruits of all your crops; then your barns will be filled to overflowing, and your vats will brim over with new wine."
--(Proverbs 3:9-10)

sure, but are their lives truly fulfilling? Probably not. There is a man who lives in a big house down the street from me. His name is Mack and he has been successful in Wall Street and selling stocks.

Mack is a multimillionaire who lives in this huge house with many sports cars, and so on and so forth. One day, I thought I'd introduce myself to the guy. From the moment he answered the door I could tell he was miserable. I got a chance to speak with him about how he became wealthy. He told me he hit it big with some good stocks and invested at the right time.

To me, it seemed like he had it all figured out; the cars, the house, and lots of money in the bank. Then I asked how his family life was doing. He said, "Not very well actually. My wife just left me, I can't stand the kids, and one of my businesses is currently going bankrupt. Mack said, "My life is falling apart one piece at a time!"

I was shocked when I heard this because he hides all these feelings so well from everyone. As far as I could tell, he seemed happy and was always smiling and having a good time. But internally he was empty and alone. He discovered that he couldn't buy his wife

"Moreover, when God gives any man wealth and possessions, and enables him to enjoy them to accept his lot and be happy in his work, this is a gift of God. He seldom reflects on the days of his life because God keeps him occupied with gladness of heart."
--(Ecclesiastes 5:19-20)

and kids back. He came to the realization that all these materialistic things were only a temporary fix. Mack was longing for something else. He was reaching out for love.

"Whoever loves money never has enough; whoever loves wealth is never satisfied with his income."
--(Ecclesiastes 5:10)

"Do not wear yourself out to get rich; have the wisdom to show restraint. Cast but a glance at riches, and they are gone, for they will surely sprout wings and fly off to the sky like an eagle."
--(Proverbs 23:4-5)

What mattered most was the love of his family, and love and acceptance from his peers.

If you are not a good person without money, then you will never be any good with it. If God decides to bless you with a generous income, or with any form of income, make sure you are making wise decisions with it. In all reality it's His anyway!

Everything you have in your life is not because "you" got it. It's not because "you" earned it. It's God's money, and He can

In Matthew 25:29 it says,

"For everyone who has will be given more, and he will have abundance. Whoever does not have, even what he has, will be taken from him."

> *"He who gathers money little by little makes it grow."*
> *--(Proverbs 13:11)*

"But godliness with contentment is great gain. For we brought nothing into the world, and we can take nothing out of it. But if we have food and clothing, we will be content with that. People who want to get rich fall into temptation and a trap and into many foolish and harmful desires that plunge men into ruin and destruction. For the love of money is a root of all kinds of evil. Some people, eager for money, have wandered from the faith and pierced themselves with many griefs."
--(1 Timothy 6:6-10)

take it away faster than you can think, if you are not spending it wisely.

> *"Life is a succession of lessons, which must be lived to be understood."*
> *--Ralph Waldo Emerson*

"But remember the Lord your God, for it is He who gives you the ability to produce wealth." --(Deuteronomy 8:18)

"The blessings of the Lord brings wealth, and He adds no trouble to it." --(Proverbs 10:22)

It's amazing to see how relevant these 2000 year old verses are today. I think the *Big Guy* might know what He's doing!

UNFINISHED BUSINESS

Don't leave any unfinished business in your life. There was a young man named Tom who was struggling with many things that most teenage boys do while growing up. He tended to be a little on the mean side and didn't treat others with respect. His father quickly took notice and was concerned. His father tried everything he could to help Tom. He even offered to give him the keys to his Porsche if he would turn his life around.

The deal was that if he could get good grades, go to church, and read his Bible every single day, he would hand over the keys to the Porsche. However, Tom remained stubborn throughout the next few months. His grades did improve and he did attend church. But the deal was to complete all three of those things, and he never read his Bible. In fact, he never even picked it up. Tom threw his Bible in the closet, never to be opened again.

Later in life he got married and moved into a new house. When Tom reached the age of sixty he was going through some of his old childhood possessions. At the bottom of the pile he discovered his Bible that his father had told him to read when he was young. He suddenly noticed that something had been taped to the last page. It was the key to his father's Porsche!

Just imagine how Tom felt. He went through his whole life never knowing what his father had given him. He went through all this, simply due to his arrogance and pride.

WAR

Omar N. Bradley once said,

"Ours is a world of nuclear giants and ethical infants. We know more about war than we know about peace, more about killing than we know about living. We have grasped the mystery of the atom and rejected the Sermon on the Mount."

How do we end war? How do we end the war going on in our country? The wars between our friends and family? The war going on in Iraq is a spiritual war, one religion against another.

There is one particular story that I like about a possible solution to end war. There is a man named Dan who fought in this war against terrorism and served his country for many years. He was also in a business that helped people gain a generous income and obtain financial freedom. His business dealt with people, as all businesses do, but one of the people within his business was fighting for the enemy. Dan was a sniper, and set to line up his shot, when all of a sudden he noticed that the very man he was trying to kill was actually in his business!

Philippians 4:13 says,

"I can do all things through Christ which strengthens me."

There's no possible way Dan could kill this man! First of all, the man had a wife and kids, just as he did. Second, it was one of his closest friends from the business. And last, the very same man he was trying to kill was one of his biggest down-line! The point is, get people in your business! And if you believe in God, then bring others to Him. And bring them fast!

THE ROCK

Throughout the Bible we see how God uses some of the worst people "the scum of the earth," to fulfill His purpose. I was intrigued by the life of Pastor Miles McPherson of the Rock Church. When Miles was growing up, he was headed down a path of darkness. Throughout his teen years he was into all sorts of drugs, marijuana, cocaine, and somehow trouble always seemed to find him.

Miles had attended church several times, but it didn't seem to make any sense to him. He was an exceptional athlete and even went on to play professional football for the San Diego Chargers. This doesn't sound like it ended up all that bad for Miles, but he was still empty inside, still searching for more. For some reason there remained a huge void in his life.

Miles soon had to quit playing football due to a major injury. What now? Where would he go from here, and what did God have in store for his life? He joined Skyline Church and was desperately searching for answers. Miles began to counsel with the pastor, and it quickly changed his life. He discovered what his purpose was in life, to lead people to Christ. Miles wasn't the greatest speaker, but he knew God was calling him to ministry.

> *"We are pressed on every side by troubles, but not crushed and broken. We are perplexed because we don't know why things happen as they do, but we don't give up and quit. We are hunted down, but we get up again and keep going."*
> *--(2 Corinthians 4:8-9)*

God spoke to him and told him he needed to become a pastor and change lives. Through patience, hard work, and faith, Miles has now led thousands of people to the Lord. God has given him the ability to reach out and connect with thousands throughout San Diego and even the world. He formed the Rock Church in San Diego and is spreading the Word of God at an incredible rate. He has taken a new and exciting approach in sharing the *Good News*. Miles has the ability to connect with both the young and old in a truly miraculous way.

How did he transform and go from a lost and confused young teenager to an amazing pastor who has changed the lives of many? The answer is God! God can take anyone, no matter what their background, and use them for good. One of the greatest ways to connect with people is through personal experience and testimony. Miles allowed God to guide his heart, and it has not only changed his life, but the lives of so many others!

1 Peter 4:8-11 says, "Above all, keep your love for one another at full strength, since love covers a multitude of sins. Be hospitable to one another without

complaining. Based on the gift they have received, everyone should use it to serve others, as good managers of the varied grace of God. If anyone speaks, his speech should be like the oracles of God; If any serves, his service should be from the strength God provides, so that in everything God may be glorified through Jesus Christ. To him belong the glory and the power forever and ever. Amen."

ONE DOOR CLOSES, ANOTHER ONE OPENS

My father has influenced me in so many positive ways. A lot of my drive and determination in life comes from him. He has had his share of mistakes, but still has a big heart.

Growing up, he had dreams of becoming a professional football player. When he was in grade school, he wanted to play Pop Warner, but his parents wouldn't sign the papers that allowed him to play. Nor would they fork out the money for him to join. Even as a youngster my father was determined to not only make the team, but be a leader.

He knew he needed money to play, so he collected Coke bottles. Each bottle was worth ten cents and he collected enough bottles to pay for Pop Warner, then forged the application, just so he could play.

He wanted to play so badly he did whatever it took. As he grew up, my father was a phenomenal athlete and played football all throughout high school. During his junior year, there were scouts at the second to last game of the season who came to watch some of the players. That day he kicked a 62 yard punt, which impressed the scouts. This was good enough to earn him a full scholarship to Purdue University.

However, in a play-off game, he was in as a running back and got hit in the knee and suffered a career ending injury. He lost not only his football scholarship, but his dream.

What was he going to do now? Football was over and it was the only thing he knew. He had dreams of playing football professionally, but this injury was bad enough to wipe that dream away. For almost two years he was depressed. He would sit in his room, set apart from the rest of the world. Month after month he would complain and do nothing with his life.

Then one day his brother walked into his room and said, "Brian, get your butt off that couch and do something with your life!" He then threw a black gym bag onto his bed. My father opened the bag and found a racquetball racket and a membership card.

He just laughed and said, "What am I going to do with this? I don't know the first thing about racquetball." But he decided it was time to do something, so he went to the local gym and began to hit the ball around. He figured he was a pretty good athlete, and his knee was almost healed, so he could probably be good at it.

While he was practicing, a man from up above was watching him. The man said, "Hey, do you mind if I play ya?" My dad said, "Yeah, but I'm not very good, and I sure as heck don't know what I'm doing out here." But being the competitor he is, he decided to play the man.

This guy absolutely destroyed him on the court 15-0, 15-1, 15-0. Now, just a side note. My father hates to lose! He is the most competitive person I know. So obviously this event didn't go well. He was furious after losing and bolted off the court.

From there he left the gym as fast as he could and threw the gym bag with the racket inside it in the trash. As he was getting into his car, a boy came running up to him. The boy said, "Hey you know who that guy is don't you?" My father said, "No, and honestly I don't care." The boy then told him that the guy he just played was ranked number 9 in the world and is name is Jeff Bowman!

After hearing that, my father grabbed the bag he had just thrown away and ran back inside. He went up to Jeff and said, "If I meet you here every single day, will you teach me?" Jeff said, "I guess I could use someone to practice on." Three years later my dad was asked to join the pro racquetball tour. He was a tremendous athlete and determined to succeed.

My father had found a new dream, and that was being a professional racquetball player. He played in the league for a total of eight years and at one point, was ranked eleventh in the world. After retiring in 1992 he now owns his own company.

Not bad for a guy who only a few years earlier didn't even know

Henry Ford once said,

"Obstacles are those frightful things you see when you take your eyes off your goal."

> *"Do you not know that the runners in a stadium all race, but only one receives the prize? Run in such a way that you may win."*
> *--(1 Corinthians 9:24)*

what racquetball was. The point I'm making is, always continue to move forward. Don't confuse slowing down with stopping.

When you work hard, new doors will open. When those doors open, take advantage of those new opportunities.

Time for Change

Point to Remember: One door closes, another door opens.

Quote to Remember: "Life is a succession of lessons, which must be lived to be understood." --Ralph Waldo Emerson

Question to Consider: How can I change to make my future better?

PERSONAL APPLICATION:

Write down any area in your life that needs improvement. What are some things you would like to change about yourself?

Facing Giants

A)

B)

C)

D)

7 *One Nation Under God*

"Now the works of the flesh are manifest, which are these; adultery, fornication, uncleanness, lasciviousness, idolatry, witchcraft, hatred, variance, emulations, wrath, strife, seditions, heresies, envying, murders, drunkenness, revellings, and such like they which do such things shall not inherit the kingdom of God."

(Galatians 5:19-21)

OUR FUTURE IN DANGER

The road to darkness in our society has already begun. God is rapidly being taken out of schools. Teachers can no longer say "Mother and Father." They can no longer say "you're a boy or girl." (You can be whatever you want). Teachers are teaching that gay marriage is fine and totally acceptable. Look at the direction our nation is taking. Where are we headed?

It is time to take it back! The devil has twisted people's minds into destroying everything our nation was founded upon. He's destroying everything our founding fathers worked so hard to keep. It is no longer time to sit around and do nothing. We had to fight for our freedom and independence before, and now we're going to have to do it again! The time to take it back is now! Do not forget your heritage. Do not forget God!

OUR FOUNDING FATHERS

The following was taken from <u>America: We Have Not Forgotten</u> and our founding fathers.

[Anytime religion is mentioned within the confines of government today, people cry separation of church and state. Our U.S. Constitution was founded on the biblical principles. It was the intention of the authors for this to be a Christian nation. The constitution had 55 people work upon it, 52 of which were evangelical Christians. We can go back at history and look at what the founding fathers wrote to know where they were getting their ideas. 94% of all quotes used by our founding fathers were based upon the Bible.

Woven into the fabric of our nation, from the very beginning was our faith. Our faith in God, and our faith in the Lord Jesus Christ. It has always been there at the very center, at the very core. What was driving them was their underlying conviction, that it was God's divine providence that we become

Thomas Jefferson wrote,

"The reason that Christianity is the best friend of government is because Christianity is the only religion that changes the heart."

> *"We want to declare a day of Thanksgiving and give honor to God for the land that He has given us."*
> *--William Bradford*

a nation; that we could experience liberty, because freedom was more than just a dream. It was something that our founding fathers truly believed was a gift from God for all men.]

"If we don't have the proper fundamental moral background, we will finally end up with a totalitarian government which does not believe in the right for anybody except the state." President Harry S. Truman

Benjamin Franklin said, "We are to never start a meeting without prayer. And when we pray, we pray for wisdom and guidance."

"Providence has given to our people the choice of their rulers, and it is the duty as well as privilege and interest of a Christian nation to select and prefer Christians for their rulers." --Chief Justice of the Supreme Court: John Jay (Now, that would not be a politically correct statement today.)

"We cannot govern ourselves outside the rule of the 10 commandments. We were never meant to do that outside of that rule." --James Madison

> *"We want our nation to be a stepping stone to take the gospel to the nations of the world."*
> *--Early Pilgrim, Unknown*

The fundamental basis of this nation's law was given to Moses on the mount and the teachings we get from Exodus, Isaiah, Paul, and Matthew.

Thomas Jefferson made it clear that there be no national religion or a wrong or right way to worship God. In fact his letter said, "Separation of church and state was taken affirmed first amendment rights." How are people reaching back and getting that?

The overall intent of our founding fathers was that we be a light and beacon of hope to all other nations. They took ideas from the Bible and incorporated them into our government. I don't see how anyone could believe that the intent was to separate church and state. If that was the case, they never would have taken the principles straight from the Bible. Nowhere in the Constitution, Bill of Rights, or the Declaration of Independence does it say there should be a separation of church and state.

"It is the duty of nations as well as men, to own their dependence upon the over-ruling power of God. And to recognize the sublime truth announced in the Holy scriptures and proven by all history that these nations only are blessed who's God is the Lord."
--Thomas Jefferson

The intent of our founding fathers was that the purposes, lessons, and principles of God's word would *never* be separated from government. Not the other way around! The whole point is that we would be influenced

"The only thing necessary for the triumph of evil, is for good men to do nothing."
--Edmond Burke

and guided by the Word of God. That we would stand up for integrity and honesty. We cannot let ourselves be deceived or disengaged.

Faith, both as a people and a nation, is what made this country great! Faith is what has been at the center and the very core of our nation. Our focus has been to have liberty, freedom, and compassion for the world. Why else would we go to battle on foreign soil? But to help every man, woman, and child have freedom. As a nation we are driven by the conviction that God created all men to be free.

COLORS OF THE WORLD

Why is racism even an issue? Why do some blacks hate whites and vice versa? Why is it always a constant battle between all the colored people of the world? This is absolutely ridiculous! I mean, just think about how boring life would be with just one race. You should be thanking God there is so much diversity and colors of the world. Throughout time there have been incredible leaders in our country of all races. Some of the greatest minds have come from all parts of the world. Think of all the inventions and ideas that have come from all over. Think of the varieties of foods, cultural styles, and diversity we have. This is a good thing!

I know one thing for sure, and that is I can't live without carne asada burritos, orange chicken, and pizza. I love burgers and all, but seriously, thank God for variety. Think of all the famous athletes like Michael Jordan, Muhammad Ali, Tiger Woods, Albert Puljos, and Pele. This list goes on and on. People from around the world have taken sports to the highest of levels. Think of all the comedians and entertainers we have like Jamie Fox, Chris Rock, and Will Smith. These people have a God-given ability to make people laugh and bring joy to others.

We have been influenced and encouraged by people of all races. Think of Miles McPherson and how many lives he has brought to the Lord. We all are here, no matter what color, to fulfill God's purpose. He created all of us to be different. That was his intention! Everyone has something to offer and bring to the table. God blessed *all* people with many different gifts and talents. It is important that we use these talents for Him.

MILLENNIUM DEVELOPMENT GOALS

As you can imagine, we face difficult situations in our homes, at work, and in our societies. But what are some of the major issues going on in the world? What are we doing to help the poor and the suffering? The United Nations has come up with eight goals to improve global living. The UN Millennium Development Goals include:

Goal 1: Eradicate extreme poverty and hunger
- Reduce by half the proportion of people living on less than a dollar a day.
- Reduce by half the proportion of people who suffer from hunger.

Goal 2: Achieve universal primary education
- Ensure that all boys and girls complete a full course of primary education.

Goal 3: Promote gender equality and empower women
- Eliminate gender disparity in primary and secondary education, preferably by 2005, and at all levels by 2015.

Goal 4: Reduce child mortality
- Reduce by two-thirds the mortality rate among children under five.

Goal 5: Improve maternal health
- Reduce by three quarters the maternal mortality ratio.

Goal 6: Combat HIV/AIDS, Malaria and other diseases
- Halt and reverse the spread of HIV/AIDS.
- Halt and reverse the incidence of Malaria and other major diseases.

Goal 7: Ensure environmental sustainability
- Integrate the principles of sustainable development into country policies and programs; reverse loss of environmental resources.
- Reduce by half the proportion of people without sustainable access to safe drinking water.

- Achieve significant improvement in lives of at least 100 million slum dwellers, by 2020.

Goal 8: Develop a global partnership for development

- Develop further and open trading and financial system that is rule-based, predictable and non-discriminatory, includes a commitment to good governance, development, and poverty reduction-nationally and internationally.
- Address the least developed countries' special needs. This includes tariff and quota-free access for their exports; enhanced debt relief for heavily indebted poor countries; cancellation of official bilateral debt; and more generous official development assistance for countries committed to poverty reduction.
- Address the special needs of landlocked and small island developing States.
- Deal comprehensively with developing countries' debt problems through national and international measures to make debt sustainable in the long term.
- In cooperation with the developing countries, develop decent and productive work for youth.
- In cooperation with pharmaceutical companies, provide access to affordable essential drugs in developing countries.
- In cooperation with the private sector, make available the benefits of new technologies, es-

pecially information and communication technologies.

One Nation Under God

Point to Remember: Our nation was founded upon the teachings from the Bible.

Quote to Remember: "The only thing necessary for the triumph of evil, is for good men to do nothing." --Edmond Burke

Question to consider: Where is our nation headed?

PERSONAL APPLICATION:

What are some things you're doing to help your community, city, and our nation?

Is there even anything?

A)

_____

_____

_____

_____

_____

_____

B)

C)

8 *The Bucket List*

"I have come that they may have life, and that they may have it more abundantly."

(John 10:10)

THE BUCKET LIST

What is The Bucket List? The Bucket List is writing down all the things you want to accomplish in life before you kick the bucket. All the goals and dreams you would like to have achieved before you croak. What would you do with your life if you found out you only had three months left to live? What would you like to have done before you die? Don't let life keep you from truly living.

Live life the way it was intended to be lived. Cherish each moment

"Time is a companion that goes with us on a journey. It reminds us to cherish each moment, because it will never come again. What we leave behind is not as important as how we have lived."
--Captain Jean-Luc Picard

because you don't know if it will be your last. You don't know when a friend or family member is going to pass on. Make sure that you always tell people you love them. Make sure the last thing they hear out of your mouth on this earth is *I love you*. Don't take anything for granted. Thank God for every single breath you take.

"For you created my inmost being; you knit me together in my mother's womb. I praise You because I am fearfully and wonderfully made; your works are wonderful, I know that full well."
--(Psalm 139:13-14)

DISCOVERING YOUR STRENGTHS

Everyone is dealt a certain hand of cards in life. Some are blessed with athletic abilities. Some are blessed at writing. Others are blessed with creative and artistic talents. Everyone is different. It is necessary that everyone is created different, because how else would the world operate?

You need some people to be laborers, some to be accountants, some to be teachers. That diversity is necessary to carry out life. So how do we discover what our strengths are? How do we know what direction we are supposed to take in life? How can we use the cards (gifts) we're given to carry out God's purpose?

One way to find out what your gifts are is to take a spiritual gifts test. This will allow you to discover what

1 Peter 4:10-11 says,

"Each one should use whatever gift he has received to serve others, faithfully administering God's grace in its various forms."

you will be good at in the future. This will also help guide you as to how you can benefit others, while earning an income at the same time. You can also take a personality or job test. These tests will ask you a series of questions, then form a hypothesis in showing where your strengths are.

As you get older, you should already have an idea what your interests and strengths are. If you are given the gift of helping others get through their problems, then you may want to become a counselor. If you are good at sports, then you may want to be a coach. If you are good at speaking in front of people, you may want to be a public speaker.

"There are different kinds of gifts, but the same Spirit. There are different kinds of service, but the same Lord. There are different kinds of working, at the same God works all of them in all men."
--1 Corinthians 12:4-6)

Whatever you are good at, use your talents to fulfill God's purpose. If you see an area that needs improvement, then work on those areas. If you're not good at public speaking, take a class that can help you improve on your speaking skills. If you struggle at confronting others, then find someone who can help you. You can do anything you set your mind to. The only one stopping you is *you*!

"Every good and perfect gift is from above coming down from the Father of the heavenly lights."
--James 1:17)

POWER OF TESTIMONY

Rick Warren wrote, "You may not be a Bible scholar, but you are the authority on your life, and it's hard to argue with personal experience. Actually, your personal testimony is more effective than a sermon, because unbelievers see pastors as professional salesmen, but see you as a 'satisfied customer,' so they give you more credibility."

You should write down the major life lessons you have learned and then share them with others. It's a good thing Solomon did this because we now have the books of Proverbs and Ecclesiastes. These books, among many others, are filled with practical lessons on living. Think about this for a second. Try and imagine

Romans 6:23 says,

"For the wages of sin is death, but the gift of God is eternal life in Christ Jesus our Lord."

how much wasted stress could have been avoided had we learned from each other's life lessons.

MAKING THE RIGHT DECISION

Sometimes it's tough to make the right decision, especially when you have to miss out on something that you know will be exciting.

A man named Brian Johnson came to my university and shared an excellent story about the importance of making the right decision. He began to tell us that he just recently turned eighteen and some buddies wanted him to go down to Tijuana, Mexico to go partying. This obviously sounded like a lot of fun, but he knew Mexico only meant trouble. He knew his parents would be upset, and the school he attended didn't allow drinking.

Brian took a lot of time contemplating the situation. Have fun and risk getting into trouble, or stay at home and be safe, but not miss out on a good time? At any age, especially eighteen, this decision is extremely tough. His buddies pushed him to go with them for hours and hours. Finally, at the last minute while he was on the way to get into the car and go with them, he changed his mind. He knew it would be best if he stayed home. He was miserable the whole time he was home.

"He who seeks good finds good will, but evil comes to him who searches for it."
--(Proverbs 11:27)

Only a few hours later, Brian received a call from one of his buddies who told him that two of his friends got into a fight and were arrested. Many of you know Mexico is not the place to go to jail. It's their own country, and they can do whatever they want with you. It turns out the two friends were locked up for an entire month, were beaten, and nearly starved. The friend who didn't get arrested had to pull out two thousand dollars to bail them out.

> *"Let your eyes look straight ahead, fix you gaze directly before you. Make level paths for your feet and take only ways that are firm. Do not swerve to the right or the left; keep your foot from evil."*
> *--(Proverbs 4:25-27)*

The lesson here is quite obvious. Make the right decisions! Go with your gut instinct on things. You're given a good conscience for a reason. Use it!

COUNSELING

One of the biggest influences in my life has been Pastor Miles. He told a great story about how to counsel people the right way. Miles said he was at a local football game when a man recognized him from across the way. The man ran up to him and said, "Hey, Pastor Miles, I was wondering if you could help counsel me

> *"Whatever is at the center of our life will be the source of our security, guidance, wisdom, and power."*
> *--Stephen Covey*

> *"True religion is real living; living with all one's soul, with all one's goodness and righteousness."*
> *--Albert Einstein*

because my life is falling apart. My wife and kids don't respect me anymore, and I can't figure out how to put all the pieces back together."

Miles said, "I'm gonna make this short and sweet." He asked the man two things. 1) Do you read your Bible every single day? The man said, "Well, no, not exactly." 2) Do you tell your wife and kids that you love them every single day? The guy said, "Well, no, not every day." Miles told the man to do those two things every single day for one month, then come back and talk.

A month later the man spotted Miles at the championship game. He went running at full speed with an enormous smile on his face, and said "That was it! My relationship with my wife is extraordinary. It took a complete turnaround. And my relationship with my kids is amazing!" As I mentioned before, put God at the center of your life and everything will begin to fall into place.

CHARISMA

> *"Some cause happiness wherever they go; others, whenever they go."*
> *--Oscar Wilde*

What is it about certain people that others tend to gravitate toward? What is it about certain people that everybody wants to be around? Charisma! People are drawn like magnets, to someone who is charismatic, joyful, and enthusiastic about life. These are the characteristics that attract others.

> *"Service is what life is all about."*
> *--Marian Wright Edelman*

I would like to share a story about the most charismatic person I have ever known, my grandfather. It is incredible to see the impact he has had on his friends, family, and everyone else who has had the privilege of meeting him. People listen to every single word he says. They have an unbelievable amount of respect for him. Why is this? Because he makes everyone feel like they are the most important thing in the world! He shows an infinite amount of love and interest in others.

When I was growing up he took me to just about every single practice, game, and event I had going on. Not only did he attend all my events, but he attended all my cousins' events as well. Keep in mind that he has thirteen grandchildren! He is a man who lives for others. This 'charisma' means more to me than words can explain. Not only does he talk the talk, but he walks the walk. If he says he will be somewhere, he will be there. The greatest way to show your love for another is by your actions.

> *"A pessimist sees the difficulty in every opportunity; an optimist sees the opportunity in every difficulty."*
> *--Sir Winston Churchill*

> *"A pint of sweat saves a gallon of blood."*
> *--General George S. Patton*

I remember a time when I was sixteen years old and was working at the batting cages. He walked in and visited with me for a bit. The cages where busy that day, but I noticed after he was done talking to me he went up to random strangers. There was a man who was teaching his son the proper mechanics of hitting, and my grandfather walked up to them. A few minutes later they were all laughing together, and it appeared as if he had known them for years. The man had his arm around my grandfather and continued laughing and joking with him.

When my grandfather came back up to the front desk where I was standing, I asked if he knew who those people were. He said, "No, but I do now!" This made a huge impact on my life because I knew I wanted to be just like that someday. He knows how to make a connection with everyone. My grandfather would talk to someone until he found out their joys and passions in life.

> *"Life is short, but there is always time enough for courtesy."*
> *--Ralph Waldo Emerson*

If I were to make a list of all the people who loved my grandfather, it would be the never-ending list! I would have to kill a rainforest to cut down enough trees to get enough paper to write all their names down! By the end of the day he got to know every single person in that room. My grandfather understands that a life lived for others, is a successful life. He says, "There is an unbelievable amount of joy that comes from helping others."

Addison Walker once said,

"It is not true that nice guys finish last. Nice guys are winners before the game even starts."

I truly believe that our purpose on this earth is to help and care for others. Life is much more fulfilling when we take the focus off of ourselves and onto others.

The Bucket List

Point to Remember: Look for the opportunity in every difficulty.

Quote to Remember: "Whatever is at the center of our life will be the source of our security, guidance, wisdom, and power."
　　　　　　　　--Stephen Covey

Question to Consider: What's on your bucket list?

PERSONAL APPLICATION:

What's on your Bucket List? What would you like to have accomplished in this life before you pass on?

A)
_____
_____

B)
_____
_____

C)
_____
_____

D)
_____
_____

E)
_____
_____

F)
_____
_____

G)

H)

9 Walkin' On Holy Water

"For God so loved the world, that He gave His only begotten Son, that whosoever believes in Him should not perish, but have everlasting life. For God sent not his son into the world to condemn the world; but that the world through Him might be saved."

(John 3:16)

LISTENING WHEN GOD SPEAKS

One of the most difficult challenges we have to face in this life is our faith. Humans struggle with religion and finding the truth on a daily basis. I am going to spend some time in this chapter dealing with how to face this *giant*.

Ralph Waldo Emerson once said,

"A believer is never disturbed because other persons do not yet see the fact which he sees."

So how and when does God speak to us? Does God even speak to us at all? The question is, are you really listening? God speaks to us in many ways, but if you aren't willing to listen, you won't hear Him. One of the biggest ways He communicates to us is through others. Often a friend or family member will give advice, guidance, and direction in your life.

You may have experienced a time in your life when you feel like you've hit rock bottom. Maybe you got fired from a job, lost a loved one, or are struggling with the battles of life. Suddenly someone pops into your life. Maybe they are there as a supportive friend. Quite possibly a complete stranger helps you out even though you don't know them. Don't look at anything as coincidence.

Christians look at life as a miracle and God speaking to them through others. You know that little voice in your head? Yeah, that's called your conscience. Why do we have this conscience? Number one, so you know He is there. Number two, so you know how to treat others. Also, so you know how to decipher what is right and what is wrong.

Our conscience is an imprint of God on our hearts. When you were younger, nobody taught you how to lie. No one ever taught you the right way to stretch the truth. But somehow, some way you knew it was wrong. What is that? It's God!

But be careful, because when we continue to push this voice aside, it will begin to fade away. When this happens, you're in trouble. You're basically telling God I don't care what you say or I don't care what you want

> *"I do not feel obliged to believe that the same God who has endowed us with sense, reason, and intellect has intended us to forgo their use."*
>
> *--Galileo*

me to do; I'm going to continue doing my own thing. You are no longer allowing Him to be your compass in life.

So if God is not the guidance in your life, who is? We are also given a conscience for our protection. In the same manner we are given rules and commandments to obey. This sounds like a rough deal, but in all reality it is for our safety and protection. He is not telling us don't do certain things for His mere satisfaction. He is telling us these things to keep us safe.

For example, Deuteronomy contains all the laws given to man by God. One of the laws says; do not cook your meat in goat milk. Now what on earth does this have to do with us today? And why would He give us such a weird law? Scientists did a study on what would happen if you ate meat that had been cooked in goat milk. They discovered there is a certain type of bacteria carried in the milk, and you can get extremely sick.

Another example God gives us is don't go to the bathroom anywhere close to where you live and sleep. Well, it's obvious. You probably don't want to see or be around it anyway. But the importance of not going to the bathroom near where you sleep is because this is exactly how toxins and disease are spread. The point is, no matter what God tells us to do, just trust him. He is trying to protect us.

PLACE OF SECURITY

As mentioned earlier in the book, many humans like to remain in their comfort zones and have that sense of security. So how do we face this giant many humans often get stuck in? Let's use the mice in the maze example. There are two mice placed into a maze, and they are in search for food.

One day a scientist placed a large piece of cheese down one of the corridors. The mice know that they need to eat soon, otherwise they might starve to death. While on the pursuit for cheese they use their instincts. The mice use their excellent sense of smell and speed to rapidly move through the maze to find their food each day. The scientist places the cheese in the exact same place every day for two weeks. The mice continue to go to that same spot because they know that the cheese will be there.

On the first day of the third week, the scientist moves the cheese into another corridor. For the next few days, the mice are confused because they continue to go to the place where they know their food will be, but it is no longer there. Mice, unlike humans, do not remain in the same place of security. Most humans would continue to go to that same place hoping the food will eventually return. The mice however, know that they must make changes and venture out into the unknown to find their food. Eventually they found the new location of the cheese and came to discover that

Matthew 7:7 says,

"Ask, and it shall be given you; seek, and you shall find; knock, and it shall be opened unto you."

there is a wide array of new and different types of cheese.

I'm trying to stress two important concepts here. First is that mice instinctively know that they need to find food for survival and know exactly what to do when the time comes. And secondly humans like to remain in a state of comfort, even when things get bad. However, both animals and humans have, in some form or another, the imprint of God. Animals already know what to do, and God gave humans the ability to know what to do as well. We have common sense for a *reason*. And God gave us all the information we need to know, both in our hearts and through reading His word!

BIG FISH

If you know exactly how and when you're going to die, how would you live your life? There is a scene in the movie Big Fish that paints a perfect picture. In the movie there is a group of four friends, and they hear a rumor that there is a witch who lives in an old rusty house at the end of the street. She was a scary lady, but rumor had

Dorothy Thompson once wrote,

"Only when we are no longer afraid do we begin to live."

it that she could foretell the future. She had a glass eye, and if you looked into her eye you could see how you die. You could see the exact age and moment you pass on. These four friends didn't believe it, and of course had to check it out.

One day they knocked on her door. When she answered, three of the kids ran off and were too scared to look. But one of the boys wanted to know how he would die and if all this was true. So when she opened the door the boy looked into her eye and saw that he would die in his sleep, but not until he was about ninety years old.

What is the point I'm trying to get across? The boy knew he wasn't going to die in the near future. He knew he would live to be at least ninety. When you know how long you're going to live, and know where you're going when you die, you tend to live your life much differently. There is nothing in this life to be feared, only understood.

BLESSINGS

Surrender to God and He will bless you. Don't get in the way of God's blessings for your life. You are the one messing it up for yourself, and no one else. If you're not blessed, it's because of you! What is it going to take to motivate you? Possibly God's wrath, His punishment, or maybe His love.

I wouldn't recommend continuing your sinful ways, just to test God and see if He is going to punish you. Because of your stubbornness, you're blocking His blessings for you, and sometimes it takes discipline and consequences for correction. Sooner or later, everything will eventually be brought to the light.

Stay "flat-lined" and let nothing phase you. For example, when you eat properly all throughout the day, you will maintain energy and feel great. There will be no extreme "ups" or "downs" if you are doing the right things. Stay consistent! Remain faithful and God will reveal what He has planned for your life over time.

Don't be half hearted either. Be sold out for God! We are nothing without Him. Learn something new every single day. Always keep your heart and mind open for what he is saying to you. Seek God, and he will be there. God wants you to know and walk with Him. He wants to be there to hold your hand through every situation in life.

Give everything up (your life) to God. Put your struggles and joys in His hands, and remember He is all! "As a faithful donkey, you will see the unseen warnings." Pray about things that are unclear to you and soon they will become crystal clear. "As a faithful donkey, you will take action that is not being taken." Turn the light in your life on, and darkness will flee. And it will flee fast!

FAITH

Life is hard enough with all the struggles we have to endure on a daily basis. You must have faith in yourself, faith in others, and most importantly faith in God. Take a look at your check-book and where you spend your money. This is a good indicator to show you what is at the center of your life.

If you're spending a lot of time and money on things that aren't helping others, and only for self-benefit, you're probably headed for trouble. If you're spending time with the wrong crowd, this is also recipe for disaster. Even if you are a good person, sooner or later you will slip. If you're a person who doesn't normally drink, but you hang out with people who do, eventually you will be doing it, too. Bad friends can be your worst enemy and lead you down the wrong path.

Oliver Wendell Homes wrote,

"It's faith in something and enthusiasm for something that makes a life worth living."

FACING GIANTS

So when we are are crushed on all sides by the giants of life, where do we turn? What do we do? We *live*, we *learn*, and we **love**…

I truly hope this book helped give some guidance and direction in your life. We face difficult times in our homes, in our jobs, and even as a nation. But that doesn't mean we can't experience the joys of life. That doesn't mean we should give up on our hopes and dreams. Remember, you are always prepared for battle. Your weapons are every lesson you have learned along the way. And lastly, look for the *opportunity* in every opposition.

> ## Walkin' On Holy Water
>
> **Point to Remember:** Seek and you shall find.
>
> **Quote to Remember:** "I am the way and the truth and the life. No one comes to the Father except through me." --(John 14:6)
>
> **Question to consider:** What is at the center of your life?

PERSONAL APPLICATION:

How has God worked in your life? What miraculous things have happened and what are the major turning points in your life?

A)
_____
_____

_____
_____

B)

C)

D)

Key Words

"Nothing is impossible with God."

(Luke 1:37)

- **Strength:** The quality or state of being strong; bodily or muscular power. Mental power, force, or vigor. Moral power, firmness, or courage. Power by reason of influence, authority, resources, numbers, etc.

- **Determination:** The act of coming to a decision or of fixing or settling a purpose. The quality of being resolute; firmness of purpose. A fixed purpose or intention.

- **Persistence:** Continued existence or occurrence. The continuance of an effect after its cause is removed.

- **Dream:** Something of an unreal beauty, charm, or excellence. An aspiration; goal.

- **Goal:** The result or achievement toward which effort is directed; aim; end. The terminal point in a race.

- **Vision:** The act or power of anticipating that which will or may come to be: *prophetic vision; the vision of an entrepreneur.* A scene, person, etc., of extraordinary beauty.

- **Perseverance:** Steady persistence in a course of action, a purpose, a state, etc. Especially in spite of difficulties, obstacles, or discouragement.

- **Motivation:** The act or an instance of motivating. The state or condition of being motivated. Something that motivates; inducement; incentive.

- **Teamwork:** Cooperative or coordinated effort on the part of a group of persons acting together as a team or in the interests of a common cause.

- **Leader:** A person or thing that leads. A guiding or directing head.

- **Accountability:** The state of being accountable, liable, or answerable.

- **Friendship:** The state of being a friend; association as friends: *to value a person's friendship.* A friendly relation or intimacy. Friendly feeling or disposition.

Life Quotes

LIFE

"Victory goes to the player who makes the next-to-last mistake."
    (Chessmaster Savielly Grigorievitch Tartakower)

"If a man does his best, what else is there?"
    (General George S. Patton)

"I find that the harder I work, the more luck I seem to have."
    (Thomas Jefferson)

"Whether you think that you can, or that you can't, you are usually right."
    (Henry Ford)

"Don't stay in bed, unless you can make money in bed."
    (George Burns)

"If you are going to get through hell, keep going."
    (Sir Winston Churchill)

"I have not failed. I've just found 10,000 ways that won't work."
(Thomas Alva Edison)

"It's kind of fun to do the impossible."
(Walt Disney)

"Obstacles are those frightful things you see when you take your eyes off your goal."
(Henry Ford)

"I'll sleep when I'm dead."
(Warren Zevon)

"Every day I get up and look through the Forbes list of the richest people in America. If I'm not there, I go to work."
(Robert Orben)

"Opportunities multiply as they are seized."
(Sun Tzu)

"The average person thinks he isn't."
(Father Larry Lorenzoni)

"Sometimes it is not enough to do our best; we must do what is required."
(Sir Winston Churchill)

"A pessimist sees the difficulty in every opportunity; an optimist sees the opportunity in every difficulty."
>(Sir Winston Churchill)

"A pint of sweat saves a gallon of blood."
>(General George S. Patton)

"It's not the size of the dog in the fight, it's the size of the fight in the dog."
>(Mark Twain)

"When you win, say nothing, when you lose, say less."
>(Paul Brown)

"It is not true that nice guys finish last. Nice guys are winners before the game even starts."
>(Addison Walker)

"The principle of life is that life responds by corresponding; your life becomes the thing you have decided it shall be."
>(Raymond Charles Barker)

"And in the end, it's not the years in your life that count. It's the life in your years."
>(Abraham Lincoln)

"Life is a process of becoming, a combination of states we have to go through. Where people fail is that they wish to elect a state and remain in it. This is a kind of death."
> (Anais Nin)

"Dost thou love life? Then do not squander time, for that the stuff life is made of."
> (Benjamin Franklin)

"Three passions have governed my life: The longings for love, the search for knowledge, And unbearable pity for the suffering of [humankind]."
> (Bertrand Russell)

"Time is a companion that goes with us on a journey. It reminds us to cherish each moment, because it will never come again. What we leave behind is not as important as how we have lived."
> (Captain Jean-Luc Picard)

"Our lives are like a candle in the wind."
> (Carl Sandburg)

"Only when we are no longer afraid do we begin to live."
> (Dorothy Thompson)

"I could not, at any age, be content to take my place by the fireside and simply look on. Life was meant to be lived. Curiosity must be kept alive. One must never, for whatever reason, turn his back on life."
(Eleanor Roosevelt)

"A useless life is an early death."
(Goethe)

"Be not afraid of life. Believe that life is worth living, and your belief will help create the fact."
(Henry James)

"Be glad of life because it gives you the chance to love, to work, to play, and to look up at the stars."
(Henry Van Dyke)

"Remember that no man loses any other life than this which he now lives, nor lives any other than this which he now loses."
(Marcus Aurelius)

"Men for the sake of getting a living forget to live."
(Margaret Fuller)

"Study as if you were going to live forever; live as it you were going to die tomorrow."
(Maria Mitchell)

"Nothing in life is to be feared. It is only to be understood."
(Marie Curie)

"Twenty years from now you will be more disappointed by the things you didn't do than by the ones you did do. So throw off the bowlines. Sail away from the safe harbor. Catch the trade winds in your sails. Explore. Dream. Discover."
(Mark Twain)

"There was never yet an uninteresting life. Such a thing is an impossibility. Inside of the dullest exterior there is a drama, a comedy and a tragedy."
(Mark Twain)

"Let us so live that when we come to die even the undertaker will be sorry."
(Mark Twain)

"An individual has not started living until he can rise above the narrow confines of his individualistic concerns to the broader concerns of all humanity."
(Martin Luther King, Jr.)

"Reading is the basic tool in the living of a good life."
(Mortimer Adler)

"Many people die with their music still inside them. Why is this so? Too often it is because they are always getting ready to live. Before they know it, time runs out."
(Oliver Wendell Holmes)

"To live is the rarest thing in the world. Most people exist, that is all."
(Oscar Wilde)

"Write it on your heart that every day is the best day in the year. No man has learned anything rightly, until he knows that every day is Doomsday."
(Ralph Waldo Emerson)

"Life is a succession of lessons, which must be lived to be understood."
(Ralph Waldo Emerson)

"Life is a progress, and not a station."
(Ralph Waldo Emerson)

"Life is short, but there is always time enough for courtesy."
(Ralph Waldo Emerson)

"Life is 'trying things to see if they work."
(Ray Bradbury)

"The purpose of life is a life of purpose."
(Robert Byrne)

"Lives, like money, are spent. What are you buying with yours?"
(Roy H. Williams)

"Our care should not be to have lived long as to have lived enough."
(Seneca)

"Half our life is spent trying to find something to do with the time we have rushed through life trying to save."
(Will Rogers)

"Not everything that can be counted counts, and not everything that counts can be counted."
(Albert Einstein)

"A lie gets halfway around the world before the truth has a chance to get its pants on."
(Sir Winston Churchill)

"The artist is nothing without the gift, but the gift is nothing without the work."
(Emile Zola)

"The full use of your powers along lines of excellence."
(Definition of "happiness" by John F. Kennedy)

"In the End, we will remember not the words of our enemies, but the silence of our friends."
(Martin Luther King Jr.)

"Problems worthy of attack prove their worth by fighting back."
(Paul Erdos)

"Good people do not need laws to tell them to act responsibly, while bad people will find a way around the laws."
(Plato)

"Whenever I climb I am followed by a dog called 'Ego.'"
(Freidrich Nietzsche)

"Never interrupt your enemy when he is making a mistake."
(Napoleon Bonaparte)

"Human history becomes more and more a race between education and catastrophe."
(H.G. Wells)

"Talent does what it can; genius does what it must."
(Edward George Bulwer-Lytton)

"He who has a 'why' to live, can bear with almost any 'how.'"
(Friedrich Nietzsche)

"I'm all in favor of keeping dangerous weapons out of the hand of fools. Let's start with typewriters."
(Frank Lloyd Wright)

"Some cause happiness wherever they go; others, whenever they go."
(Oscar Wilde)

"I shall not waste my days in trying to prolong them."
(Ian L. Fleming)

"When you do the common things in life in an uncommon way, you will command the attention of the world."
(George Washington Carver)

"Once you eliminate the impossible, whatever remains, no matter how improbable, must be the truth."
(Sherlock Holmes)

"A people that values its privileges above its principles soon loses both."
(Dwight D. Eisenhower)

"The significant problems we face cannot be solved at the same level of thinking we were at when we created them."

(Albert Einstein)

"Many a man's reputation would not know his character if they met on the street."

(Elbert Hubbard)

"Perfection is achieved, not when there is nothing more to add, but when there is nothing left to take away."

(Antoine de Saint Exupery)

"Knowledge speaks, but wisdom listens."

(Jimi Hendrix)

"A witty saying proves nothing."

(Voltaire)

"I have often regretted my speech, never my silence."

(Xenocrates)

"There are people in the world so hungry, that God cannot appear to them except in the form of bread."

(Mahatma Gandhi)

"When you gaze long into the abyss, the abyss also gazes into you."
(Friedrich Nietzsche)

"Everyone is a genius at least once a year; a real genius has his original ideas closer together."
(George Lichtenberg)

"Success usually comes to those who are too busy to be looking for it."
(Henry David Thoreau)

"While we are postponing, life speeds by."
(Seneca)

"Wise men made proverbs, but fools repeat them."
(Samuel Palmer)

"It has become appallingly obvious that our technology has exceeded our humanity."
(Albert Einstein)

"The secret of success is to know something nobody else knows."
(Aristotle Onassis)

"Any man who is under 30, and is not a liberal, has not heart; and any man who is over 30, and is not a conservative, has no brains."
(Sir Winston Churchill)

"When I am working on a problem I never think about beauty. I only think about how to solve the problem. But when I have finished, if the solution is not beautiful, I know it is wrong."
(Buckminster Fuller)

"Make everything as simple as possible, but not simpler."
(Albert Einstein)

"Forgive your enemies, but never forget their names."
(John F. Kennedy)

"He who hesitates is a damned fool."
(Mae West)

"If I were two-faced, would I be wearing this one?"
(Abraham Lincoln)

"You can get more with a kind word and a gun than you can with a kind word alone."
(Al Capone)

"I have never let my schooling interfere with my education."
(Mark Twain)

"Always do right- this will gratify some and astonish the rest."
(Mark Twain)

"A scholar who cherishes the love of comfort is not fit to be deemed a scholar."
(Lao Tzu)

"The best way to predict the future is to invent it."
(Alan Kay)

"The only thing necessary for the triumph of evil is for good men to do nothing."
(Edmund Burke)

"If stupidity got us into this mess, then why can't it get us out?"
(Will Rogers)

"The right to swing my fist ends where the other man's nose begins."
(Oliver Wendell Holmes)

"Whatever is begun in anger ends in shame."
(Benjamin Franklin)

"We are not retreating – we are advancing in another direction."
(General Douglas McArthur)

"The man who does not read good books has no advantage over the man who cannot read them."
(Mark Twain)

"The truth is more important than the facts."
(Frank Lloyd Wright)

"There are only two ways to live your life. One is as though nothing is a miracle. The other is as though everything is a miracle."
(Albert Einstein)

"Life is a process of becoming, a combination of states we have to go through. Where people fail is that they wish to elect a state and remain in it. This is a kind of death."
(Anais Nin)

"Dreams pass into the reality of action. From the actions stems the dream again; and this interdependence produces the highest for of living."
(Anais Nin)

"Three passions have governed by life: The longings for love, the search for knowledge, and unbearable pity for the suffering of [humankind]."
(Bertrand Russell)

"Time is a companion that goes with us on a journey. It reminds us to cherish each moment, because it will never come again. What we leave behind is not as important as how we lived."
(Captain Jean-Luc Picard)

"There are as many nights as days, and the one is just as long as the other in the year's course. Even a happy life cannot be without a measure of darkness, and the word 'happy' would lose its meaning if it were not balanced by sadness."

(Carl Jung)

"Ours is a world of nuclear giants and ethical infants. We know more about war than we know about peace, more about killing than we know about living. We have grasped the mystery of the atom and rejected the Sermon on the Mount."

(Omar N. Bradley)

"The truth is always exciting. Speak it, then. Life is dull without it."

(Pearl S. Buck)

"Our care should not be to have lived long as to have lived enough."

(Seneca)

MOTIVATIONAL

"Sportsmanship for me is when a guy walks off the court and you really can't tell whether he won or lost, when he carries himself with pride either way."

(Jim Courier)

"You miss 100% of the shots you don't take."
(Wayne Gretzky)

"The only one who can tell you 'you can't' is you. And you don't have to listen."
(Nike)

"Accept challenges so that you may feel the exhilaration of victory."
(Unknown)

"It does not matter how many times you get knocked down, but how many times you get up."
(Vince Lombardi)

"Excellence is not a single act but a habit. You are what you do repeatedly."
(Shaquille O'Neal)

"I can accept failure. Everyone fails at something. But I can't accept not trying."
(Michael Jordan)

"I can't play being mad. I go out there and have fun. It's a game, and that's how I am going to treat it."
(Ken Griffey, Jr.)

"In the end, it's extra effort that separates a winner from second place. But winning takes a lot more than that, too. It starts with complete command of the fundamentals. Then it takes desire, determination, discipline, and self-sacrifice. And finally, it takes a great deal of love, fairness and respect for your fellow man. Put all these together, and even if you don't win, how could you lose?"
(Jesse Owens)

"Gold medals don't make champions.. Hard work does."
(Unknown)

"Winning as a team is better than anything. It's great to share success."
(Jim Harbaugh)

"Good coaches teach respect for the opposition, love of completion, the value of trying your best, and how to win and lose graciously."
(Brooks Clark)

"Half this game is ninety percent mental."
(Yogi Berra)

"It's lack of faith that makes people afraid of meeting challenges, and I believed in myself."
(Muhammad Ali)

"You got to be careful if you don't know where you're going, because you might not get there."
(Yogi Berra)

"We didn't lose the game; we just ran out of time."
(Vince Lombardi)

"If everything seems under control, you're just not going fast enough."
(Mario Andretti)

"If you win through bad sportsmanship, that's no real victory."
(Babe Didrikson Zaharias)

FAITH

"True religion is real living; living with all one's soul, with all one's goodness and righteousness."
(Albert Einstein)

"God didn't promise us smooth sailing, but He did promise us a safe landing."
(Unknown)

"It's faith in something and enthusiasm for something that makes a life worth living."
(Oliver Wendell Holmes)

"A believer is never disturbed because other persons do not yet see the fact which he sees."
(Ralph Waldo Emerson)

"An authentic life is the most personal form of worship. Everyday life has become my prayer."
(Sarah Ban Breathnach)

"It is in our lives and not our words that our religion must be read."
(Thomas Jefferson)

"These, then, are my last words to you: Be not afraid of live. Believe that life is worth living, and your belief will help create the fact."
(William James)

"I do not feel obliged to believe that the same God who has endowed us with sense, reason, and intellect has intended us to forgo their use."
(Galileo Galilei)

"I don't know why we are here, but I'm pretty sure that it is not in order to enjoy ourselves."
(Ludwig Wittgenstein)

"I am ready to meet my Maker. Whether my Maker is prepared for the great ordeal of meeting me is another matter."
(Sir Winston Churchill)

"You can only find truth with logic if you have already found truth without it."
(Gilbert Keith Chesterton)

"It was the experience of mystery – even if mixed with fear – that endangered religion."
(Albert Einstein)

"Wise men make proverbs, but fools repeat them."
(Samuel Palmer)

FRIENDSHIP

"A friendship founded on business is better than a business founded on friendship."
(John D. Rockefeller)

"Be nice to people on your way up because you will meet them on your way down."
(Jimmy Durante)

"The true measure of a man is how he treats someone who can do him absolutely no good."
(Samuel Johnson)

"If you haven't anything nice to say about somebody, come sit next to me."
(Alice Roosevelt Longworth)

"Love is friendship set on fire."
(Jeremy Taylor)

"We make a living by what we get, but we make a life by what we give."

(Winston Churchill)

"Where there is love there is life."

(Mohandas K. Gandhi)

Biblical Quotes

SUCCESS

"And now I will show you the most excellent way."
(1 Corinthians 12:31)

"Do not let this Book of Law depart from your mouth; meditate on it day and night, so that you may be careful to do everything written in it. Then you will be prosperous and successful."
(Joshua 1:8)

"He was with him and gave him success in everything he did."
(Genesis 39:3)

"In everything you do, put God first, and he will direct you and crown your efforts with success."
(Proverbs 3:6)

"May He give you the desire of your heart and make all your plans succeed."
(Psalm 20:4)

"Commit to the Lord whatever you do, and your plans will succeed."

(Proverbs 16:3)

GOALS, VISIONS, & DREAMS

"In the last days God will pour out His Spirit on all people and they will prophesy, see visions and dream dreams. Thus, the Holy Spirit will be a transporter of dreams and visions from God."

(Acts 2:17)

"Your word is a lamp to my feet and a light for my path."

(Psalm 119:105)

"Nothing is impossible with God."

(Luke 1:37)

"I tell you the truth, if you have faith as small as a mustard seed, you can say to this mountain, 'Move from here to there' and it will move. Nothing will be impossible for you."

(Matthew 17:20)

"Delight yourself in the Lord and He will give you the desires of your heart."

(Psalm 37:4)

"Though you have not seen Him, you love Him; and even though you do not see Him now, you believe in Him and are filled with an inexpressible and glorious joy, for you are receiving the goal of your faith, the salvation of your souls."

(1 Peter 1:8-9)

"The goal of this command is love, which comes from a pure heart and a good conscience and a sincere faith."

(1 Timothy 1:5)

"So we make it our goal to please Him, whether we are at home in the body or away from it."

(2 Corinthians 5:9)

"Whatever your hand finds to do, do it with all your might."

(Ecclesiastes 9:10)

AWARENESS

"Folly delights a man who lacks judgment, but a man of understanding keeps a straight course."

(Proverbs 15:21)

"We should go up and take possession of the land, for we can certainly do it."

(Numbers 13:30)

"So as he thinks within himself, so he is."
(Proverbs 23:7)

"The wisdom of the prudent is to give thought to their ways."
(Proverbs 14:8)

RELATIONSHIPS

"For out of the outflow of the heart the mouth speaks."
(Matthew 12:34)

"But let everyone be quick to hear, slow to speak and slow to anger."
(James 1:19)

"Let your conversation be always full of grace, seasoned with salt, so that you may know how to answer everyone."
(Colossians 4:6)

"Words from a wise man's mouth are gracious, but a fool is consumed by his own lips."
(Ecclesiastes 10:12)

"Through patience a ruler can be persuaded, and a gentle tongue can break a bone."
(Proverbs 25:15)

"Do not let any unwholesome talk come out of your mouths, but only what is helpful for building others up according to their needs, that it may benefit those who listen."
(Ephesians 4:29)

"Pleasant words are a honeycomb, sweet to the soul and healing to the bones."
(Proverbs 16:24)

"A gentle answer turns away wrath, but a harsh word stirs up anger."
(Proverbs 15:1)

"How great is the love the Father has lavished on us, that we should be called children of God! And that is what we are! The reason the world does not know us is that it did not know Him. Dear friends, now we are children of God, and what we will, has not yet been make known. But we know that when He appears, we shall be like Him, for we shall see Him as He is. Everyone who has this hope in Him purifies himself, just as He is pure."
(1 John 3:1-3)

"We are commanded in Scripture to love our neighbor as ourselves."
(Mark 12:31)

"For I will forgive their wickedness and will remember their sins no more."
(Hebrews 8:12)

"My command is this: Love one another as I have loved you. Greater love has no one than this, that one lay down his life for his friends."
(John 15:12-13)

CHOICES

"He who seeks good finds good will, but evil comes to him who searches for it."
(Proverbs 11:27)

"Let your eyes look straight ahead, fix you gaze directly before you. Make level paths for your feet and take only ways that are firm. Do not swerve to the right or the left; keep your foot from evil."
(Proverbs 4:25-27)

"I have resolved that my mouth will not sin."
(Psalm 17:3)

"A man of knowledge uses words with restraint, and a man of understanding is even-tempered."
(Proverbs 17:27)

"Each one should test his own actions. Then he can take pride in himself, without comparing himself to somebody else, for each one should carry his own load."

(Galatians 6:4)

"He who is faithful in a very little thing is faithful also in much; and he who is unrighteous in a very little thing is unrighteous also in much."

(Luke 16:10)

FAITH

"Faith is the substance of things hoped for, the evidence of things not seen."

(Hebrew 11:1)

"God hath dealt to every man the measure of faith."

(Romans 12:3)

"Without faith it is impossible to please him; for he that cometh to God must believe that he is, and that he is a rewarder of them that diligently seek him."

(Hebrews 11:6)

"For by grace are you saved through faith; and that not of yourselves: it is the gift of God."

(Ephesians 2:8)

> "Cast not away therefore your confidence (faith), which hath great recompense of reward."
>
> (Hebrews 10:35)

> "For as the body without the spirit is dead, so faith without works is dead also."
>
> (James 2:26)

> "Knowing this, that the trying of your faith worketh patience."
>
> (James 1:3)

> "That the trial of your faith, being much more precious than of gold that perisheth, though it be tried with fire, might be found unto praise and honor and glory at the appearing of Jesus Christ."
>
> (1 Peter 1:7)

> "What things you desire, when you pray, believe that you receive them, and you shall have them."
>
> (Mark 11:24)

> "According to your faith be it unto you. Thy faith has made thee whole."
>
> (Matthew 9:29,22)

> "I have fought a good fight. I have finished my course, I have kept the faith."
>
> (2 Timothy 4:7)

CRISIS

"We are pressed on every side by troubles, but not crushed and broken. We are perplexed because we don't know why things happen as they do but we don't give up and quit. We are hunted down, but we get up again and keep going."
(2 Corinthians 4:8-9)

"Because you know that the testing of your faith develops perseverance. Perseverance must finish its work so that you may be mature and complete, not lacking anything."
(James 1:2-4)

"Resist the devil, he will flee from you. Draw near to God, and he will draw near to you."
(James 4:7,8)

"Casting all your care upon him; for he cares for you."
(1 Peter 5:7)

"It is necessary to pass through many troubles on our way into the kingdom of God."
(Acts 14:22)

"Do you not know that the runners in a stadium all race, but only one receives the prize? Run in such a way that you man win."
(1 Corinthians 9:24)

BELIEF

"In the beginning was the Word, and the Word was with God, and Word was God.
>   (John 1:1)

"So God created man in His own image, in the image of God He created him; male and female He created them."
>   (Genesis 1:27)

"But God demonstrates His own love for us in this: While we were still sinners, Christ died for us."
>   (Romans 5:8)

"For in this hope we were saved. But hope that is seen is no hope at all. Who hopes for what he already has?
>   (Romans 8:24)

"For God so loved the world that He gave His one and only son, that whoever believes in him shall not perish but have eternal life."
>   (John 3:16)

"Trust in the Lord with all your heart; and lean not unto your own understanding. In all thy ways acknowledge him, and he shall direct thy paths."
>   (Proverbs 3:5,6)

DISCIPLESHIP

"The Word of God is living and active. Sharper than any double edged sword, it penetrates even to dividing soul and spirit, joints and marrow; it judges the thoughts and attitudes of the heart."
(Hebrews 4:12)

"The tongue has the power of life and death, and those who love it will eat its fruit."
(Proverbs 18:21)

"The mouth of the righteous is a fountain of life."
(Proverbs 10:11)

"But you are a chosen people, a royal priesthood, a holy nation, a people belonging to God, that you may declare the praises of Him who called you out of darkness into His wonderful light."
(1 Peter 2:9)

"And now these three remain: faith, hope and love. But the greatest of these is love."
(1 Corinthians 13:13)

FUNDAMENTALS

"But the plans of the Lord stand firm forever, the purposes of His heart through all generations."
(Psalm 33:11)

"Do not think of yourself more highly than you ought, but rather think of yourself with sober judgment, in accordance with the measure of faith God has given you."

(Romans 12:3)

"What, then, shall we say in response to this? If God is for us, who can be against us? He who did not spare His own Son, but have Him up for us all – how will He not also, along with Him, graciously (or freely) give us all things? Who will bring any charge against those whom God has chosen? It is God who justifies. Who is he that condemns? Christ Jesus, who died – more than that, who was raised to life – is at the right hand of God and is also interceding for us. Who shall separate us from the love of Christ? Shall trouble or hardship or persecution or famine or nakedness or danger or sword? …No, in all these things we are more than conquerors through Him who loved us. For I am convinced that neither death nor life, neither angels nor demons, neither the present nor the future, nor any powers, neither height nor depth, nor anything else in all creation, will be able to separate us from the love of God that is in Christ Jesus our Lord."

(Romans 8:31-39)

"Therefore be careful how you walk, not as unwise men, but as wise, making the most of your time, because the days are evil."

(Ephesians 5:15-16)

"For thou art my rock and my fortress; therefore for thy name's sake lead me and guide me."

(Psalms 31:3)

"For as many as are led by the Spirit of God, they are the sons of God."

(Romans 8:14)

"Your attitude should be the same as that of Christ Jesus."

(Philippians 2:5)

TRAINING

"Train yourself to be godly. For physical training is of some value, but godliness has value for all things, holding promise for both the present life and the life to come."

(1 Timothy 4:7-8)

"Dear friends, this is now my second letter to you. I have written both of them as reminders to stimulate you to wholesome thinking."

(2 Peter 3:1)

"Therefore, I urge you, brothers, in view of God's mercy, to offer your bodies as living sacrifices, holy and pleasing to God – which is your spiritual worship."

(Romans 12:1-2)

"Teach us to number our days aright, that we might gain a heart of wisdom."

(Psalm 90:12)

MONEY

"Bring the whole tithe into the storehouse, that there may be food in My house. Test me in this,' says the Lord Almighty, 'and see if I will not throw open the floodgates of heaven and pour out so much blessing that you will not have room enough for it. I will prevent pests from devouring your crops, and the vines in your fields will not cast their fruit."

(Malachi 3:10-11)

"Honor the Lord with your wealth, with the first fruits of all your crops; then your barns will be filled to overflowing, and your vats will brim over with new wine."

(Proverbs 3:9-10)

"He who gathers money little by little makes it grow."
(Proverbs 13:11)

"For everyone who has will be given more, and he will have an abundance. Whoever does not have, even what he has will be taken from him."
(Matthew 25:29)

"But remember the Lord your God, for it is He who gives you the ability to produce wealth."
(Deuteronomy 8:18)

"The blessings of the Lord brings wealth, and He adds no trouble to it."
(Proverbs 10:22)

"Do not wear yourself out to get rich; have the wisdom to show restraint. Cast but a glance at riches, and they are gone, for they will surely sprout wings and fly off to the sky like an eagle."
(Proverbs 23:4-5)

"Better one handful with tranquility than two handfuls with toil and chasing after wind."
(Ecclesiastes 4:6)

"Whoever loves money never has enough; whoever loves wealth is never satisfied with his income."
(Ecclesiastes 5:10)

"Moreover, when God gives any man wealth and possessions, and enables him to enjoy them to accept his lot and be happy in his work – this is a gift of God. He seldom reflects on the days of his life, because God keeps him occupied with gladness of heart."

(Ecclesiastes 5:19-20)

"But godliness with contentment is great gain. For we brought nothing into the world, and we can take nothing out of it. But if we have food and clothing, we will be content with that. People who want to get rich fall into temptation and a trap and into many foolish and harmful desires that plunge men into ruin and destruction. For the love of money is a root of all kinds of evil. Some people, eager for money, have wandered from the faith and pierced themselves with many grief's."

(1 Timothy 6:6-10)

PERFORMANCE

"Plans to prosper you and not to harm you, plans to give you hope and a future."

(Jeremiah 29:11)

"I can do everything through Him who gives me strength."

(Philippians 4:13)

"I press on toward the goal to win the prize for which God has called me heavenward in Christ Jesus."
(Philippians 3:14)

GIVING THANKS

"For you created my inmost being; you knit me together in my mother's womb. I praise You because I am fearfully and wonderfully made; your works are wonderful, I know that full well."
(Psalm 139:13-14)

"Rejoice in the Lord always. I will say it again: Rejoice!"
(Philippians 4:4)

"God be gracious to us and bless us, and cause His face to shine upon us. That Thy way may be known on the earth, Thy salvation among all nations."
(Psalm 67:1-2)

"I have come that they may have life, and that they may have it more abundantly."
(John 10:10)

GAME PLAN

"For I know the plans I have for you,' declares the Lord, 'plans to prospers you and not to harm you, plans to give you hope and a future."
(Jeremiah 29:11)

"A simple man believes anything but a prudent man gives thought to his steps." "those who plan what is good find love and happiness."
(Proverbs 14:15 & 22)

"Many are the plans in a man's heart, but it is the Lord's purpose that prevails."
(Proverbs 19:21)

"Search me, O God, and know my heart; try me, and know my thoughts: And see if there be any wicked way in me, and lead me in the way everlasting.. I know that thou cast do everything, and that no though can be withholding from thee."
(Psalm 139:23)

"Create in me a clean heart, and renew a right spirit in me."
(Job 42:2)

"Let the words of my mouth, and the meditation (thoughts) of my heart, be acceptable in thy sight, O Lord, my strength, and my redeemer."
(Psalm 19:14)

FALSE PROPHETS

"Have no fellowship with the unfruitful works of darkness but rather reprove them."

(Ephesians 5:11)

"Neither is there salvation in any other; for there is no other name under heaven given among men, whereby we must be saved."

(Acts 4:12)

"Believe not every spirit, but try spirits whether they are of God: because many false prophets are gone out into the world.. Every spirit that confesses not that of Jesus Christ is come in the flesh, is not of God."

(1 John 4:1-3)

"These are written that ye might believe that Jesus is the Christ, the Son of God; and that believing ye might have life through his name.. and he that believeth not shall be damned."

(John 20:31)

HEAVEN

"In the beginning God created the heavens and the earth."

(Genesis 1:1)

"Then I saw a new heaven and a new earth, for the first heaven and the first earth had passed away, and the sea existed no longer. I also saw the Holy City, new Jerusalem, coming down out of the heaven from God, prepared like bride adorned for her new husband. Then I heard a loud voice from the throne: Look! God's dwelling is with men, and He will live with them. They will be His people, and God Himself will be with them and be their God. He will wipe away every tear from their eyes. Death will exist no longer; grief, crying, and pain will exist no longer, because the previous things have passed away."

(Revelation 21:1-4)

"Then the One seated on the throne said, 'Look! I am making everything new.' He also said, 'Write, because these words are faithful and true.' And He said to me, 'It is done! I am the Alpha and the Omega, the Beginning and the End. I will give to the thirsty from the spring of living water as a gift. The victor will inherit these things, and I will be his God and he will be My son. But the cowards, unbelievers, vile, murderers, sexually immoral, sorcerers, idolaters, and all liars – their share will be in the lake that burns with fire and sulfur, which is the second death."

(Revelation 21:5-8)

"He carried me away in the Spirit to a great and high mountain and showed me the holy city, Jerusalem, coming down out of heaven from God, arrayed with God's glory. "

(Revelation 21:10-11)

"The city had a massive high wall, with 12 gates. Twelve angels were at the gates, names were inscribed, the names of the 12 sons of Israel. There were three gates on the east, three gates on the north, three gates on the south, and three gates on the west. The city wall had 12 foundations, and on them were the 12 names of the Lamb's 12 apostles."

(Revelation 21:12-14)

"The city is laid in a square; its length and width are the same. He measured the city with the rod at 12,000 stadia. Its length, width, and height are equal. Then he measured its wall, 144 cubits according to human measurement, which the angel used. The building material of its wall was jasper, and the city was pure gold like clear glass."

(Revelation 21:16-19)

"The foundations of the city wall were adorned with every kind of precious stone: jasper, sapphire, emerald, etc."

(Revelation 21:19-20)

"The 12 gates are 12 pearls; each individual gate was made of a single pearl. The broad street of the city was pure gold, like transparent glass."

(Revelation 21:21)

"The city does not need the sun or the moon to shine on it, because God's glory illuminates it, and its lamp is the Lamb. The nations will walk in its light, and the kings of the earth will bring their glory into it."

(Revelation 21:23-24)

"Each day its gates will never close because it will never be night there. They will bring the glory and honor of the nations into it. Nothing profane will ever enter it: no one who does what is vile or false, but only those written in the Lamb's book of life."

(Revelation 21:25-27)

SALVATION

"For what is a man profited, if he shall gain the whole world, and lose his own soul? Or what shall a man give in exchange for his soul?"

(Matthew 16:26)

"For we shall all stand before the judgment seat of Christ, and every tongue shall confess to God."

(Romans 14:10,12)

"Christ Jesus came into the world to save sinners."
(1 Timothy 1:15)

"I can do all things through Christ who strengthens me."
(Philippians 4:13)

"If we confess our sins, he is faithful and just to forgive us our sins, and to cleanse us from all unrighteousness."
(1 John 1:9)

"Now the works of the flesh are manifest, which are these; adultery, fornication, uncleanness, lasciviousness, idolatry, witchcraft, hatred, variance, emulations, wrath, strife, seditions, heresies, envying, murders, drunkenness, revellings, and suck like.. they which do such things shall not inherit the kingdom of God."
(Galatians 5:19-21)

"The Lord is not willing that any should perish but that all should come to repentance."
(2 Peter 3:9)

"For God so loved the world, that he gave his only begotten Son, that whosoever believes in him should not perish, but have everlasting life. For God sent not his son into the world to condemn the world; but that the world through him might be saved."

(John 3:16)

"For the wages of sin is death; but the gift of God is eternal life though Jesus Christ our Lord."

(Romans 6:23)

Author Bio
Light At My Feet

"Let the words of my mouth, and the meditation (thoughts) of my heart, be acceptable in thy sight, O Lord, my strength, and my redeemer."

(Psalm 19:14)

PAST, PRESENT, FUTURE

I believe that sharing your personal testimony is one of the most powerful ways to reach people. You can give a first-hand account of the events and turning points experienced in life. This is exactly what I would like to share with you. I grew up in a good Christian home and loved to play sports. While I was growing up, I played soccer, basketball, hockey, and baseball.

But baseball was the one that really stuck out to me. My mom said I was born with a bat in my hands. Baseball is in my blood, I guess. Throughout my junior high and high school years I was usually the best player on all the teams that I played on. I played third base and was always batted cleanup. Sports came easy to me, and I love to play.

After high school, I was recruited by the coach at Mesa College in San Diego. Coach told me that I was the number one guy for the third base position. I was ecstatic because I was playing college ball, and I could see a bright future ahead. Since I was young, the only thing I ever wanted to do in life was play major league baseball. And I felt I had the talent.

As the end of the semester approached, right before the coach posted the roster for the upcoming season, I realized I wasn't on it. This was shocking because he told me I was the number one starter. Now, I went from going to the starter, to getting benched. I almost didn't know how to handle this because I had always been the best player on every team that I played for. This was a humbling experience, but I was still determined to play.

So after my first red shirt season at Mesa, I soon went on over to Grossmont College. Rumor had it, that they had a much better coach and baseball program. That next fall pre-season I rose to the occasion, with ten home runs and did a good job defensively. As it came time for this season's posting of the roster, I was on it, but the coach told me I would never see the field. He told me I would only go in as a DH (Designated Hitter).

So this was obviously quite frustrating and a huge wake-up call for me. I had gone from the top of the world to the bottom of the barrel. And in a hurry! I was always taught never to quit and never to give up. So I stuck with my goals and decided to press on.

The year after Grossmont, I finally found a team I could play on; Imperial Valley College in El Centro, CA. It was one hundred and twenty degrees and humid every single day. In spite of this, I simply wanted to play ball. When you want something bad enough, you will do anything to get it. And let me tell ya, this was the ultimate sacrifice. It was a huge sacrifice even to live there. I did well my first season, but there was still room for improvement. However, I was excited to be on the team and continue fulfilling my dreams.

The following season I was hit again with another letdown. I received straight A's, but failed one class. I worked hard at all my classes, but this particular class was extremely difficult. I felt that I should have received at least a C. I attended class every single day, turned in all my assignments, and studied hard for every test. Even after speaking with the teacher, he would not change my grade or allow any makeup work. This was devastating, because it was yet again another season I would not be playing.

I set out on the road again and again, finally ending up at California Baptist University. Now I had an even bigger challenge. I hadn't played in a season, got let go from two different teams (which were junior college teams), and now I'm going to try and make it onto one of the top four-year schools in the nation. I was determined and would not be shaken. I wanted to play, and that's exactly what I was going to do!

The first day of practice coach told all the players whom were trying out that they probably wouldn't make it for the mere fact that he already had too many guys on the team. On top of that, there were a hundred-plus guys trying out for the team. Talk about bad news on top of more bad news. The problems just kept coming and wouldn't let up. I worked harder than I had ever worked in my life. I was in the hospital six times throughout the fall semester.

I didn't care about anything except making that team. Rejection was no longer an option. As the last week approached, he told us that he would post the final roster. I was obviously nervous and didn't know if I could take anymore abuse. My dreams of playing ball were rapidly diminishing. I walked up to the list and couldn't believe what I was seeing. One other guy and I, out of a hundred guys, made the team! This was so exciting, and I couldn't believe what had just happened.

Then a couple of weeks before the actual season started, the biggest crises of my life arose. I had gone to visit my family over the Thanksgiving break and was throwing a football around for several hours. At the time my arm felt fantastic and I was really zipping it in there. The next day, something strange began to happen to me. My arm went numb and started tingling, as if I had been sleeping on it. As soon as I received feeling back in my right arm, I noticed a pain like no other. It was if someone was taking a dagger and stabbing it over and over again. Then suddenly it began to swell like someone blowing up a balloon.

My right arm was enormous and in an excruciating amount of pain. Without hesitation, I drove myself to the hospital. I went to the emergency room, and they immediately put me into a room. The nurse could see that there was no time to waste and I need to be looked at. The doctor ran all kinds of test on me, (Doppler test, ultrasound, drawing blood). It turns out I had *five* blood clots in my right arm. This is extremely dangerous because the clots can travel into your heart and lungs. Once this happens, you don't have much time left to live. The doctor told me, had I waited another hour, I probably would have died. My left arm measured at 17" around the bicep, and 27" around the right arm!

I was in the hospital two weeks and had a total of four surgeries. Even though I almost died, the only thing going on in my mind was this was, once again, another year I couldn't play baseball. I was absolutely devastated, depressed, sad, and lonely. This was by far the worst thing that had ever happened to me. I was only 22 years old and was told that I could have died! The doctor also told me that I would never be able to throw, let alone even be able to use my right arm again. Just imagine having all your dreams taken from you, then being told you won't even be able to use your arm. It will just be hanging there, as if just for looks or show.

Shockingly, I was thankful this had happened to me. I will explain. First, I realized how many people loved and cared for me. I never really knew how much people cared, before all this had happened. Hundreds and hundreds of people prayed for me and came in to visit me in the hospital. My mom stayed with me the entire time. I told her it was okay if she went home and at least get some sleep, but she never left my side. This meant more to me than anything in the world. Because finally I realized what matters most in this life – relationships! We are and would be nothing without other people in our lives. I realized that baseball is a great thing, but is it really the most important thing?

I think God has opened my eyes to a whole new world. After the experience I viewed life much differently. I made sure I took nothing for granted. I have begun to enjoy the smaller things in life. I thank God every day for just being alive, and having such a wonderful family. I feel for those who have lost people in their lives. I feel for the families who have to press on without their sons, daughters, mothers, fathers, etc. I appreciate all the wonderful things God has given us. I am truly grateful for everything I have been given.

I believe that if one day God wants me to play professional baseball, then I will play professional baseball. But in the meantime, I know His plan for my life. And that plan is to help others. My mission is to help people who are struggling in life. The most amazing things begin to happen when you take the focus off yourself, and onto others.

When you do this, God will begin to bless you in more ways than you can ever imagine. Life will be so enjoyable, and there will be a tremendous amount of love. All of the problems you are going through will rapidly diminish, and you will experience true joy. Problems will go away because you know that they are just trials. Every problem we face, know that God is trying to teach you something. Are you paying attention to what He is teaching you? Or are you frustrated and lose focus? Our purpose here on earth is not to live selfishly, but to live for others and be light to the world. Allow people to see God through you!

MISSION STATEMENT

My mission is to serve, to serve God, my family, my friends, and all others. I will seek to learn, grow, and fulfill God's purpose for my life. Wherever I am, and wherever I go, I want to be a light to others. My wish is that people can see love, joy, peace, and God through me. I want to be a positive influence on my family and friends. I want to bring as many people to Christ as I can, and to one day have God say, "Well done, my good and faithful servant."

Light At My Feet

Point to Remember: Life is a journey with many twists, turns, up's and down's, but when you have God, anything can be accomplished.

Quote to remember: "Sharing your personal testimony is one of the most powerful ways to reach people."

Question to Consider: What impact are you going to make?

PERSONAL APPLICATION:

What is your mission statement?

_____
_____

_____
_____

_____
_____

_____
_____

_____
_____.

AUTHOR BIO

Nick Laughter presently lives in Denver, CO. While living in San Diego, CA, he was involved with "Men With a Purpose" and the Rock Church. You'll enjoy his special blend of charisma, humor, enthusiasm, and passion. He is currently working to form the "Homeless World Series" and strives to improve the lives of others.

CONTACT INFORMATION

Website
www.FacingGiantsSite.com

Email
Facinggiantssite@gmail.com

BIBLIOGRAPHY

1) New American Standard Bible, copyright 1960, 1962, 1963, 1968, 1971, 1973, 1975, 1977 by The Lockman Foundation

2) How to Change the World, David Bornstein. Oxford University Press, August 2007.

3) Holman Christian Standard Bible, Copyright © 1999, 2000, 2002, 2003, 2005 by Holman Bible Publishers.

4) Schwab Foundation - http://www.schwabfound.org/sf/index.htm

5) Negroponte - (http://laptop.media.mit.edu/vision/index.shtml

6) America We Have Not Forgotten

Printed in the United States
149536LV00001B/1/P